Decisions Made Now Will Benefit You Later!

We all make retirement decisions, though some make them more quickly, more efficiently, more wisely than others. A safe and secure retirement begins with the foundational knowledge you can use to choose the best financial advisor, ask the right questions and take a proactive role in your retirement planning.

It is important to work with a financial advisor who is aware of the latest IRA distribution and tax rules. These rules are complicated and full of tax traps that could cost you your retirement dreams. If our current economic situation has taught us anything, choosing an educated financial advisor is essential to keeping more of your hard-earned money.

I do not sell investment products. I do not earn commissions. I simply believe that a comfortable retirement starts with accurate IRA advice. I am here to educate.

ED SLOTT'S
ELITE
IRA
ADVISOR
GROUP℠
Find an advisor
at **IRAhelp.com**

That is the message behind this guide, which will provide you with 125 essential ways to save and stretch your wealth so that you can spend your golden years how you have planned and envisioned them.

I hope you find my *Retirement Decisions Guide* educational and useful.

Ed Slott, CPA
Ed Slott and Company, LLC

CONTENTS

Chapter 1:

IRA Basics

1. Plan now and retire twice as rich

Studies show that people who become educated about their finances and play a role in planning and monitoring their IRAs wind up twice as rich as those who haven't a clue. Consider these three facts from a Dartmouth/Wharton study:

- **Wisdom pays**—Retirement planning is a strong predictor of retirement wealth. If you learn how money grows and how much you will need at retirement, you are much more likely to achieve your stated goals.

- **Money grows**—Those who plan are more likely to end up at retirement with twice the wealth of those who do not plan.

- **Start early**—Those who are financially literate when young are more likely to plan for retirement.

2. Avoid past years' mistakes

The Great Recession was painful for most IRA investors. But these valuable lessons were learned:

- **Get IRA advice.** If you are unsure what to do, consider hiring a financial advisor who understands IRA portfolio allocation, tax issues, diversification, distribution planning, hedging and emotional handholding.

- **Keep some cash.** Setting cash aside in your IRA will buffer your portfolio against downturns and let you invest when share prices are low.

- **Know your mix.** Proper allocation among stocks and bonds— and diversification among different stock and bond classes—is essential.

- **Stocks aren't certain.** Stocks are volatile, and stock-price growth comes after long periods of time. Even after 15 years, stock values can suddenly decline or remain flat for a period. Ease volatility by investing in a strategic mix of assets—such as stocks, bonds, annuities, cash, real estate and other investments.

- **Bonds have risks.** Many investors shooting for income continue to invest in individual bonds. But as we know now, any company—including "safe" ones—can go belly-up. That's why bond investments need to be highly diversified among many different types of fixed-income securities, through bond funds or individual bonds.

- **Recessions end.** While severe market downturns cause tremendous anxiety, they eventually end. That truth is hard to believe when markets are perilously low, headlines are frightening and IRA statements look foreboding. But they do.

3. What are the IRA rules for 2016?

Contribution Levels

- **Up through age 49**—$5,500 for 2016
(Visit **IRAhelp.com/2016** for all 2016 IRA and tax tables.)
- **Age 50 onward**—$6,500 for 2016
(Visit **IRAhelp.com/2016** for all 2016 IRA and tax tables.)

Conversion Eligibility

Everyone qualifies to convert a Traditional IRA or SEP IRA to a Roth IRA. After a two-year waiting period, SIMPLE IRAs can also be converted. Income restrictions on a conversion were repealed starting in 2010.

4. Do these myths sound familiar?

Many people who don't save enough in a 401(k) and IRA typically have five reasons why not. But those feel-good excuses are flawed. Here's why:

- **Myth: Taxes will be lower.** Many people believe that when they retire, their tax rates will be lower because they won't be earning as much income. But there's nothing stopping the government from raising them in future years. So withdrawals from a Traditional IRA years from now could actually face higher income taxes—even if you're not working.

- **Myth: You'll work longer.** When portfolios were down, many people shrugged and said they'll just have to work longer. Sounds good, but here's a stark fact: As you age, the odds are you physically won't be able to work as hard as you want—or as long as you once did.

- **Myth: Pensions will kick in.** As we know now, even companies that may once have been healthy sometimes end up filing for bankruptcy. Or restructure. Or face such hardships that they roll back benefits they once promised. This can include government and public pensions that were once thought to be secure.

- **Myth: Social Security starts at 62.** That's true—now. But there's nothing to say that the federal government won't raise the minimum age at which benefits start—or reduce benefits for those at specific income levels.

- **Myth: Inheritances will arrive.** Don't count on it. Many seniors are living longer today thanks to dietary changes and moderate exercise. Even when aging adults grow ill, medical care is so good that infirmities can be controlled and minimized for years. Lucky you—mom and dad will live forever!

5. Why bother saving in an IRA?

If you're contributing to a 401(k) at work, you may be wondering why you need an Individual Retirement Account (IRA). Or you may feel you can't afford to save the max in both. But opening and saving even a little in an IRA is important. Here's why:

- **Tax-free growth.** Assets in an IRA grow tax-free—meaning there are no taxes on capital gains when you sell assets within the account. Taxes are paid upon distribution.
- **Tax deduction.** You can always deduct your full Traditional IRA contribution if your modified adjusted gross income in 2016 is less than $98,000 (married filing jointly) or $61,000 (single) (visit **IRAhelp.com/2016** for all 2016 IRA and tax tables).
- **Investment freedom.** Unlike a 401(k), which typically offers a small menu of mutual funds, an IRA lets you invest in any securities you wish. In addition, you can use an IRA to diversify your total retirement portfolio by investing in assets not offered by your 401(k).
- **Long-range planning.** When you eventually leave your job, you will almost certainly wind up transferring the balance of your 401(k) into an IRA for greater investment choices, control and efficiency. You may as well open one now, even if you don't contribute the max each year.

6. What is a Traditional IRA?

The Individual Retirement Account (IRA) was created in 1974 with the enactment of the Employee Retirement Income Security Act (ERISA). The original version is commonly called a "Traditional IRA," which distinguishes it from other types of IRAs that have been introduced over the years. What you need to know about a Traditional IRA:

- **Contributions.** Each year you may contribute up to an amount set by the tax law—provided you earned at least that sum in salary or self-employment income (i.e. compensation). The max you can contribute is based on whether you are age 49 or younger—

or age 50 or older (visit **IRAhelp.com/2016** for current levels). Contributions cannot be made once you reach the year you turn age 70 ½.

- **Deadline.** Annual contributions can be made until April 15 of the following year.

- **Deduction.** If you are covered by a company plan, you can deduc your annual contribution if you meet the latest income levels (visit **IRAhelp.com/2016** for the current levels).

- **Gains.** Gains on assets in an IRA are not taxed until they are withdrawn, giving assets an enormous opportunity to compound and grow over time.

- **Withdrawals.** The Traditional IRA was created to encourage retirement savings. So withdrawals before age 59 ½ face both income tax and a stiff 10% penalty. You can withdraw penalty-free starting at age 59 ½—but withdrawals aren't mandatory. Starting at age 70 ½, you are required to take annual distributions based on the IRS' life-expectancy table.

- **Taxes.** Withdrawals face income taxes at your tax rate at the time.

- **Heirs.** The person or persons you want to receive your assets upon death should be named in your IRA beneficiary document. IRA assets shouldn't be passed through your will.

7. What is a Roth IRA?

The Roth IRA was named for William Roth, a U.S. senator from Delaware who sponsored the Taxpayer Relief Act of 1997. Here's what you need to know:

- **Qualifications.** Only taxpayers under specific income levels can open and contribute annually to a Roth IRA (visit **IRAhelp.com/2016** for the latest qualifying levels).

- **Contributions.** Each year you may contribute up to an amount set by the tax law, provided you earned at least that sum in salary or self-employment income. The max you can contribute is based on whether you are age 49 or younger—or age 50 or older (visit **IRAhelp.com/2016** for the latest levels). Annual contributions can be made at any age.

- **Deadline.** Annual contributions can be made up until April 15 of the following year.
- **Deduction.** There is no tax deduction for contributions to a Roth IRA.
- **Gains.** Gains on assets in a Roth IRA are generally not taxed, giving them an enormous opportunity to grow and compound over time.
- **Withdrawals.** Assets in a Roth IRA may be withdrawn after age 59 ½ tax-free if any Roth was opened more than five years earlier. That means every dollar growing in a Roth IRA can be yours to keep. In addition, there is no mandatory withdrawal age, meaning assets can continue to grow tax-free.
- **Penalty.** Gains withdrawn before age 59 ½ will face a 10% penalty plus taxation, as will certain pre-59 ½ distributions of converted funds.
- **Heirs.** The person or persons you want to receive your assets upon death should be named in your Roth IRA's beneficiary document. Roth IRA assets shouldn't be passed through your will.
- **Inheritance.** Upon death, a Roth IRA can pass estate-tax free to a spouse. Or it can pass to one or more non-spousal beneficiaries, though part of the assets may be needed to pay estate taxes. Non-spouse heirs must take distributions based on their life expectancies set by the IRS. But the required annual distributions are generally income-tax free. The catch is that a Roth IRA had to have been set up by the original Roth IRA owner more than five years before the distribution.

8. What is a SEP IRA?

A Simplified Employee Pension Individual Retirement Account (SEP IRA) is an IRA for the self-employed or small-business owner. The rules for a SEP IRA are the same as for a Traditional IRA (*see tip #6*)—with the following exceptions:

- **To qualify.** You must be a self-employed individual or small-business owner (with or without employees) whose venture generates income. You can open a SEP IRA even if you work for an employer and participate in another retirement plan—provided your side business generates income and complies with certain ownership guidelines.

- **Contributions.** You can contribute up to 20% of net earnings from self-employment—(25% if incorporated)—but not to exceed annual amounts set by the tax law (visit **IRAhelp.com/2016** for the latest levels). If your business has employees, all eligible employees must receive the same benefits under a SEP IRA plan. Unlike a Traditional IRA, you can continue to make contributions to your SEP IRA after age 70 ½, if you are still working for the company.

- **Taxes.** Contributions are deductible dollar for dollar. This means if you contribute $25,000 to your SEP IRA, you can deduct this amount from your income on tax returns. This feature makes SEP IRA contributions highly desirable from a retirement-planning and tax-savings standpoint.

9. Which IRA is right for you?

- **What's your income?** If your income level is under the eligibility threshold, open a Roth IRA.

- **Are you self-employed?** Open a SEP IRA and contribute up to 20% of your net income (25% if you're incorporated)—but not more than the annual amounts set by the tax law (visit **IRAhelp.com/2016** for the latest levels).

- **Do you have kids?** Open a Roth IRA for teens with salaried summer jobs. You can make the contributions on their behalf. So, if your child earned $2,000 over the summer, you can contribute up to that amount in his or her Roth IRA. They will thank you when they retire and can withdraw the accumulated assets tax-free.

10. Easy way to save $36,000

You can easily contribute at least $1,326 a year to an IRA. Here's how: The average American winds up with $5.50 in spare change each week. Pool the coins along with $20 a week in stray singles, and you'll have $1,326 by year's end. Why bother? If you continue to contribute this sum annually for 15 years, and your IRA account earns a modest 6% annually on a compounded basis, you will wind up with nearly $36,000. That's hardly chump change.

11. What is a Roth IRA conversion?

The tax code lets you convert all or part of your Traditional IRA or SEP IRA to a Roth IRA. Prior to 2010, the tax code allowed such a conversion—but only if your annual income did not exceed $100,000. But starting in 2010, this income threshold was repealed. That means anyone can convert a Traditional IRA into a Roth IRA—regardless of annual income. What you need to know:

- **Benefit:** A Roth conversion grants you all the benefits of a Roth IRA—including tax-free withdrawals of earnings after five years of ownership and after reaching age 59 ½.

- **Drawback:** You must pay income tax on the portfolio's market value on the date of conversion.

12. Does a Roth IRA conversion pay?

In many cases, the answer is a resounding yes. If you can pay the income tax due on the portfolio's market value at the time of conversion, the move is a powerful one.

- **Here's why:** Historically, today's income-tax rates are relatively low. A conversion allows you to pay income tax at the current rate and get rid of Uncle Sam for life. So, for example, if a $500,000 portfolio in a Roth IRA grows to $1 million in 15 years, all of those dollars are yours. And you get to enjoy all of the benefits of a Roth IRA, including no mandatory withdrawals.

13. Roth IRA conversion questions

Converting your Traditional IRA to a Roth IRA is a terrific deal. Anyone can do this—regardless of annual income, but you will owe income tax on the conversion. Five big questions:

- **When doesn't it pay?** If you expect your income to decline in retirement and tax rates to be where they are now, a Roth conversion might not be ideal. That's because the tax hit on your withdrawals from a Traditional IRA in the future will likely be lower than what you would have to pay now to convert.

- **How is a conversion taxed?** If you convert part or all of a Traditional IRA to a Roth IRA, you will owe income tax on the assets' market value on the date of conversion. But if you have made nondeductible IRA contributions, you have to follow the IRS' pro-rata tax rule, which can be tricky. Consult a financial advisor or an accountant with specialized knowledge in this area.

- **How to cover the tax?** Ideally you want to use funds in taxable accounts to pay the tax. It doesn't make sense to tap an IRA or 401(k) to pay taxes and a 10% early-withdrawal penalty if you're under age 59 ½.

- **Can the tax be minimized?** Sure. Convert only part of the Traditional IRA.

- **What about a SEP IRA?** Yes, you can convert part or all of a SEP IRA. If you convert the entire SEP IRA, however, you can't continue making deductible contributions to your newly created Roth IRA. Instead, you'll have to set up a new SEP IRA account for future deductible contributions.

Getting tax-free income from a Roth IRA can be rewarding, but getting there from a Traditional IRA conversion can be daunting. You'll probably owe income tax on most or all of the retirement funds you convert.

What's more, a complete conversion will often push you into a higher tax bracket. For example, consider Andrew and Bonnie, who are married and file a joint tax return. During her career, Bonnie worked at a series of companies with 401(k) plans.

Whenever Bonnie would change jobs, she'd roll the 401(k) balance into her Traditional IRA. By the time the couple reached their 50s, eyeing retirement, there was $200,000 in Bonnie's IRA.

- **Their plan:** Convert Bonnie's Traditional IRA to a Roth IRA. However, all of the money in her IRA came from pre-tax 401(k) contributions. A complete rollover would add $200,000 to Bonnie and Andrew's taxable income for the year.

  Typically, their taxable income (after deductions) is around $120,000 a year. That puts them in the 25% tax bracket.

  Another $200,000 in taxable income from a Roth IRA conversion would push them all the way through the 25% and 28% brackets, well into the 33% bracket. They might owe about $60,000 in additional federal income tax.

- **Going partial:** Instead, Bonnie decides to convert only $25,000 of her IRA this year. That would increase the couple's taxable income to $145,000, still within the 25% tax bracket for 2016. The added tax would be $6,250 (25% of $25,000), which Andrew and Bonnie can manage. Bonnie plans to implement partial Roth IRA conversions year after year, staying within a tax bracket to hold down the tax bill. Eventually, her entire Traditional IRA will be moved to the Roth side, at a relatively low tax cost over a period of years.

- **Ed Slott's advice:** A series of partial conversions will make it easier to pay the tax from a taxable account. Then your entire Traditional IRA can become a Roth IRA without a haircut for withdrawals to pay the tax bill.

14. Yes, current tax rates are low

Federal income tax rates are at historic lows. Even if you're paying a top federal rate of 39.6%, your rate is relatively low and may rise to pay for the new wave of Congressional spending and deficits. (For a look at the 2016 tax rules, see Chapter 8.) Over time, the top tax rate has been as high as 94%. Remember, Congress can change the tax rates at any time for all taxpayers or just for those who earn more than a specific level.

Year	Top Federal Income Tax Rate
2013-2016	39.6%
2003-2012	35%
2002	38.6%
2001	39.1%
1993-2000	39.6%
1991-1992	31%
1988-1990	28%
1987	38.5%
1982-1986	50%
1965-1981	70%
1964	77%
1954-1963	91%
1952-1953	92%
1946-1951	91%
1944-1945	94%

15. What's a Roth recharacterization?

A Roth IRA "recharacterization" is a Roth IRA conversion undo.

- **How it works:** Let's say you converted your Traditional IRA to a Roth IRA. You owe income tax on the value of the assets on the date of conversion. But let's say that in the same tax year, the value of the portfolio you converted tumbles significantly. You'd still owe the original income tax—even though the portfolio's value was much higher then. Not fair!

- **Solution:** If you recharacterize the Roth IRA back to a Traditional IRA, you will no longer owe the tax from the conversion. Plus you can reconvert at a later time and pay only the tax on the lower amount.

Retroactive tax relief

After you convert all or part of your Traditional IRA to a Roth IRA, you have a unique opportunity. You can recharacterize (reverse) all or part of the conversion until October 15 of the following year.

- **How it works:** Say that Doug converts a $50,000 Traditional IRA to a Roth IRA in June 2016. Doug has more than a year—until October 15, 2017—to change his mind.

  Suppose it's October 1, 2017, and Doug's Roth IRA has grown by 20% to $60,000. Doug can leave the conversion in place, happy that he has $10,000 of gains in the account that he may be able to withdraw in the future, tax-free.

  On the other hand, suppose that Doug's Roth IRA has dropped by 20% to $40,000. Naturally, Doug won't want to pay tax on a $50,000 Roth IRA conversion in order to have a $40,000 Roth IRA.

  Thus, Doug can recharacterize the entire transaction, so the $40,000 Roth IRA reverts to a Traditional IRA. Doug will owe no tax at all on the Roth IRA conversion because the recharacterization effectively reverses it.

- **Try again:** As mentioned in this example, Doug converted in 2016 and recharacterized in 2017. Then, after waiting for more than 30 days, he can reconvert this Traditional IRA to a Roth IRA, if he wishes.

  Assume that 30 days pass and, in November 2017, Doug's Traditional IRA is still worth $40,000. Doug can reconvert and owe tax on a $40,000 conversion, rather than pay tax on the original $50,000 conversion.

  If his Roth IRA keeps falling, Doug can keep recharacterizing and reconverting until he has his IRA money on the Roth side, at the lowest tax cost. Then he'll have more upside potential for future tax-free income.

- **Happier returns:** Federal income tax returns are due on April 15 each year, but you can get an automatic six-month filing extension (not a tax payment extension!) until October 15 of each year. In our example, if Doug has requested an extension and recharacterized on time, he can simply file his 2016 tax return by October 15 and ignore the entire 2016 Roth IRA conversion.

  But what if Doug had already filed his 2016 tax return by April 15, 2017, and paid tax on the $50,000 Roth IRA conversion. Can he still recharacterize that conversion?

  Yes, Doug still has until October 15, 2017 to change his mind. If he already has paid tax on the Roth IRA conversion, he can file an amended tax return, requesting a refund or a credit against future tax payments.

- **Fine points:** Suppose that Doug is pleased with his Roth IRA conversion, but not with his tax bill. In a 33% tax bracket, for example, Doug would owe $16,500 in tax on a $50,000 conversion.

  Say that Doug feels he can afford to pay no more than $10,000 in tax. In a 33% bracket, that would be approximately the tax on a $30,000 conversion: 60% of the $50,000 Doug initially converted. Thus, Doug could recharacterize 40% of his Roth IRA back to a Traditional IRA and pay less than $10,000 in tax, not $16,500. Your tax pro can handle the number crunching on a partial recharacterization, which can be daunting.

  In yet another wrinkle, suppose that Doug converts to a Roth IRA in June 2016, as above, but the market crashes in September 2016. Doug's new Roth IRA tumbles in value so he has no interest in paying tax on the initial amount. He recharacterizes immediately.

  When a Roth IRA conversion and reversal take place in the same year, the rules are a bit different. Reconversion isn't allowed until the following calendar year or more than 30 days after the recharacterization date, whichever comes later.

In our example, Doug converts in June 2016 and recharacterizes in September 2016. Now he must wait until 2017 to reconvert the same funds he recharacterized.

16. Who's your IRA beneficiary?

No matter what kind of IRA you own, request a copy of your signed beneficiary form for review. When you receive it, be sure that the people you want to inherit your IRA's assets are listed properly. Also provide your advisor and estate attorney with copies of the signed document.

- **Reason:** When you die, your IRA does not pass according to wishes in your will. Whatever IRA assets are left will pass to the person or persons named in your signed beneficiary document.

17. Inheriting an IRA: Spouse

Under the tax law, if you inherit a spouse's IRA, there are generally no estate or income taxes due—no matter how large your inheritance. But you have three choices regarding how to treat the IRA inheritance:

- **Option #1: You can roll** the inherited IRA assets into your existing IRA or one you set up in your own name.

- **Option #2: You can transfer** the inherited IRA assets into an Inherited IRA account. If your spouse was age 70 ½ or older, you must begin taking mandatory distributions by December 31 of the year following your spouse's death. If your spouse was younger than age 70 ½, you can delay distributions until your spouse would have turned age 70 ½.

- **Option #3: You can disclaim** all or part of the IRA inheritance within nine months of the IRA owner's death. You do not get to choose who is next in line to receive the disclaimed property. Instead, the assets will pass to the IRA's contingent beneficiary, as if you had died before the IRA's owner. Since the assets will be passing to a non-spouse, estate taxes may be owed based on the value of the IRA.

18. Inheriting an IRA: Non-spouse

If you inherit an IRA from a parent or someone who isn't your spouse, you have three choices:

- **Option #1: Take distributions.** Whether you inherit a Traditional IRA or a Roth IRA, you cannot roll the assets into your existing IRA as a non-spouse. Instead, you must set up an "Inherited IRA" and have the assets transferred directly in there. Rules…

  1. Begin taking minimum distributions from the Inherited IRA by December 31 of the year following the IRA owner's death.

  2. Minimum annual withdrawals are based on the IRS' Single Life Expectancy Table (visit **IRAhelp.com/2016** to view the IRS table).

- **Option #2: Take the total.** You can choose to take the full value of the inherited IRA as a lump-sum check. You will owe income tax on the sum if you inherited a non-spousal Traditional IRA. If you inherited a Roth IRA, you may owe income tax on earnings if the owner did not have any Roth IRA for at least five years.

- **Option #3: Disclaim it.** Your third option is to disclaim the inheritance within nine months of the IRA owner's death. Why would you do this? In most cases it's done to pass the inheritance to the next-in-line beneficiary who may need it more than you do. Either way, upon inheriting, you should immediately name heirs on the beneficiary form.

- **Ed Slott's advice:** Consult an IRA advisor on the appropriate choice. If you decide to take annual distributions or a lump sum from an inherited Traditional IRA, see if you can claim the IRD deduction ("income in respect of a decedent"). It's a deduction for inheritors of a Traditional IRA on which federal estate taxes were paid (*see tip #69*).

19. Did you inherit a Roth IRA?

- **If you're the spouse**—you can roll the inherited Roth IRA into your existing Roth IRA or a newly set-up Roth IRA in your own name. Then you can avoid taking distributions for life if you choose. You also can retitle the Roth IRA as your own. Either way, upon inheriting, you should immediately name heirs on the beneficiary form. When non-spouse heirs inherit from you, they will have to take required minimum distributions each year, although they can generally stretch them out over their lifetime—income-tax free.

- **If you're a non-spouse—**

    1. Begin taking minimum distributions from the inherited Roth IRA by December 31 of the year following the Roth IRA owner's death.

    2. Minimum annual withdrawals are based on the IRS' Single Life Expectancy Table (visit **IRAhelp.com/2016** to view the table). But the mandatory annual required distributions will generally be tax-free.

20. Beware of this costly IRA penalty

If you're a non-spouse who's inheriting a Roth IRA, you have to set up an "Inherited Roth IRA" to receive the assets.

- **Big trap:** Be sure to take the required minimum distribution (RMD) each year based on the IRS' life-expectancy table (visit **IRAhelp.com/2016** to view the table). If you don't take the distributions, you will owe a 50% penalty on each RMD you missed—even though the distribution remains tax-free.

21. What wealthy retirees do right

An IRA is likely to be one of your most valuable assets when you retire. While my wealthiest retired clients differ in net worth and retirement goals—all share similar behavior patterns regarding their IRAs and how they saved over time. Here are their saving secrets:

- **Get real.** Most wealthy clients who retire with sizable IRAs resisted becoming greedy over time. They set goals and maintained retirement portfolio allocations that matched their savings targets and risk tolerance levels over time. They also didn't second-guess their plan—even in 2008.

- **React smartly.** If your IRA remains properly allocated and highly diversified based on your age and goals, you have little to fear in terms of market swings. You also want to avoid the urge to invest in hot trends or go to 100% cash in a panic. Both moves often backfire.

- **Seek smart help.** Many of my clients who amassed sizable IRAs by retirement age did so with the help of a professional advisor who was educated in IRAs and tax strategies.

- **Watch carefully.** Studies show that if you plan correctly and track your spending and IRA statements, you are more likely to reach your goals. The reason is simple: If you take an interest in your money, you're more likely to care. And if you care, you're more likely to save more, spend less and invest strategically.

- **Withdraw wisely.** You want to leave assets in an IRA as long as possible—especially in retirement. Tax-deferred savings compound over time and have the best chance of greater growth. For income, you're always better off working part-time or withdrawing from taxable accounts first before tapping into your IRA.

- **Hedge risks.** We all fear unforeseen market mishaps. To guard against the impact of downturns, wealthy retirees take protective steps in their IRA portfolios and other accounts. For example, they set aside enough cash to cover emergencies, take out adequate insurance policies to protect against health and financial blows, and invest in a range of different, highly diversified investments to cushion against market setbacks.

- **Ed Slott's advice:** Most people can live comfortably on much less than they're spending now—if they find ways to spend wisely. Many wealthy retirees are happy with the little things in life and appreciate what they already own. Few overspend on cars, boats, homes or vacations. And when they do spend, they are extremely frugal.

Chapter 2:

Making Plans

22. Saving plenty isn't hopeless

No matter how much you need to save by the time you retire, never feel as though saving annually is hopeless. It's not, and even small amounts add up over time. The reason is the "compounded interest" you'll receive in tax-deferred retirement accounts like an IRA.

- **What's compound interest?** This is interest you earn not only on your initial contribution but also on accumulated amounts earned each year. Let's say you have $1,000 in an IRA investment and it earns 7% in the first year. You'll have $1,070. Now let's say that in the second year, your $1,070 earns 6%. You'll have $1,134. And so on, year after year. That's the power of compound interest.

- **Ed Slott's advice:** Set your annual IRA savings goal early in the year and find ways to reach that goal by setting aside money each week or month. Or consider having your IRA plan automatically withdraw the amount from your bank checking account each month. If the money is removed directly, you're less likely to miss it.

23. How much will you need to save?

This answer depends on how much you'll need each year for living expenses in retirement—or once you stop working full-time. How to estimate your savings goal:

- **Step 1.** Gather last month's bills, ATM slips and credit card receipts. Add them up—but leave out expenses that won't likely exist when you retire, such as college tuitions, mortgage payments, credit card debt, disability insurance premiums, etc.

- **Step 2.** Next, multiply your monthly sum by 12 for an annual total.

- **Step 3.** A dollar today will buy less in the future thanks to rising prices (inflation). So take your current annual total and see what it will be in the year you plan to retire. Use an online inflation calculator.

- **Step 4.** Subtract your estimated annual Social Security benefit and any estimated annual pension and annuity payouts. You can calculate your Social Security benefit at SSA.gov.

- **Step 5.** Now you know roughly how much income you'll need in your first year of retirement. But how many years of this income will be enough? While it's impossible to say with any certainty, you can use a life insurance company's life-expectancy table.

- **Step 6.** Multiply your annual retirement income by your years of life expectancy. The result is a rough estimate of how much you'll need to save by retirement. If it seems high, you'll have to cut back on your post-retirement living expenses. Of course, during retirement your savings will need to be invested properly so it keeps pace with inflation.

- **Step 7.** Clearly your goal is to save at least the amount you calculated. Even better is to save a sum that when invested conservatively at 5% will provide you with what you need each year, allowing you to leave your principal intact and pass as much as possible to heirs.

24. How much risk can you tolerate?

Once you know your estimated retirement age and savings goal, the next step is to evaluate how much risk you can tolerate.

> ED SLOTT'S
> **ELITE**
> ≡**IRA**≡
> **ADVISOR**
> **GROUP**™
> Find an advisor
> at **IRAhelp.com**

- **What is risk?** Risk is a fancy word for fear. As we know from the economic turmoil of 2008, markets drop, sometimes considerably. When they do, investors grow fearful as their portfolios shrink in value. If your portfolio dropped in 2008 and you worried you might not have enough years left until retirement to make back what you lost, you likely were overexposed to stocks and took on too much risk.

- **Is safety risky?** Not investing at all is also risky—particularly if you have 15 years or longer until retirement. If you stick only with conservative investments paying a low rate of return, there's a high risk that your portfolio won't grow to the amount you need.

- **Striking a balance.** Risk is about the odds of being exposed to hardship and fear. Finding the right balance between safety and satisfaction requires a little rational thought. Start by looking at how many years you have left until retirement and what rate of return will satisfy your savings goal.

- **Ed Slott's advice:** The more years remaining until retirement, the more risk your portfolio can take on for a higher rate of return. As for your personal fear factor, that's important, too. Fear should play a cautionary role as you determine an ideal rate of return over time. Fear is only a problem if fear alone dictates your investment strategy.

25. What's your asset allocation?

After you figure out when you plan to retire, how much you'll need to save, and the level of risk you can tolerate, you need to determine the ideal asset allocation of your IRA portfolio. Ideally this exercise should be done with a financial advisor who fully understands how IRAs work and the tax benefits involved.

- **What is asset allocation?** Asset allocation is how you divide your savings among stocks, bonds, cash and other investments. Asset allocation is important for two reasons: By properly allocating savings, you maximize your portfolio's growth potential and minimize the negative impact of market declines.

- **How to allocate.** Your allocation levels will depend on when your savings will be needed and the realistic rate of return you can expect over that time period.

- **What's diversification?** Once you've decided what percentage of your portfolio should be devoted to stocks and bonds, the next step is to create a diversified mix of different types of stocks and bonds. This is done to further minimize portfolio jolts over time.

26. When to rebalance a portfolio

No matter how you allocate and diversify your IRA assets now, the mix you choose is likely to become lopsided after 12 months or even sooner. That's because markets are constantly in flux, changing the values of your investments.

- **Example:** If your allocation is supposed to be 50% stocks and 50% bonds, your investment values could change by year-end. How so? A $1,000 investment today in a stock fund may be worth $1,500 at the end of the year. And $1,000 invested in a bond fund may be worth $800. Therefore, your allocation will no longer be 50%-50%, and it will need to be brought back into line.

- **When to rebalance.** Each year, revisit your IRA portfolio to see if it's still allocated and diversified the way you originally planned. If the allocation is too far off, you will need to rebalance your IRA portfolio either alone or with the assistance of a financial advisor.

- **How to rebalance.** You can rebalance two ways: You can sell your position in stock or bond investments in your IRA that exceed your original allocation and invest the proceeds in positions that are below your target percentages. Or you can invest cash in either stock or bond positions to bring the allocation into line.

27. Risks of do-it-yourself planning

While the media has done a fine job over the past 15 years simplifying investing principals for average investors, some magazines and TV shows have oversimplified retirement planning. It's a highly complex process that requires in-depth knowledge and impartiality. Here's how do-it-yourself planners get into trouble:

- **Tip tipsy**—Without someone qualified to remind you of your investment plan, you're more likely to try to capitalize on someone else's hot tip.

- **Too positive**—People who think positively are often successful in life. But they also can get into hot water with their personal finances and investing. That's because positive thinkers tend to assume that markets and their investments will always rebound. As we witnessed in 2008, even the mightiest companies can go under, and markets may not rebound fast enough.

- **Hardly objective**—If you make your own financial and investment decisions without seeking professional advice, you're not going to be objective, no matter how hard you try.

- **Lax on laws**—Educated financial advisors keep up with the tax laws that affect retirement planning. If you make a move on your own without understanding or knowing these laws, you could pay more in taxes or lose out on opportunities.

- **Slow on strategies**—New ways to invest emerge all the time. Unless you're up on the different ways to capitalize on tax loopholes, trusts, insurance, annuities and other products, you may not achieve your retirement objectives.

28. Retirement dreams vs. reality

For years, age 65 was the magic number for retirement. Today and in the future, that age may no longer be quitting time. Plan for age 65 but don't assume that work stops then. The odds are greater that work will stop sooner—or later. Here's why:

- **Sudden retirement.** As we know, many people in their 50s recently found themselves out of work for the first time in their careers during the recession. What's more, many remained unemployed for a year or longer, forcing families to live on less or dip into their savings. When these people did find employment, the jobs typically paid less than what they had been earning. The lesson: Don't assume you'll be working until age 65 or at the salary you're earning now.

- **Much later retirement.** Work used to mean manual labor, so by age 65 most people were physically tired and in need of a much slower pace. Today, many people earn a living on their computers and love what they do. As a result, they intend to continue earning income well into their 70s—either because they want to or because they need to fund some aspect of their lifestyle or the needs of their children.

- **Ed Slott's advice:** When speculating about your retirement age, don't assume too much. The odds are that retirement will come sooner than you think and that your salary in your 60s and 70s will likely be considerably less than you made in your 40s or early 50s. This is why it's so important that you save as much as possible while you're young.

29. Why a financial advisor is essential

Retirement planning is more than just saving enough money for the years when you'll be working less. There are a wide range of complicated retirement issues that need to be considered, including taxes, estate planning and insurance. To retire comfortably, you need financial help. Here's what a financial advisor who's an expert in IRAs can do for you:

- **Less anxiety.** If you hire the right financial advisor, you'll be less likely to worry day after day about whether you've done enough or too little with your investments. Once you and your advisor create a financial plan, your advisor also will help you stick to it.

- **Reduced tracking.** If an advisor has carefully thought through what you need to do and you've implemented the plan, you're less likely to monitor the Dow Jones Industrial Average or S&P 500 day after day. Those are short-term concerns. Instead, you'll be thinking long-term.

- **Size management.** Your IRA is now (or will be soon) your most valuable asset. A qualified financial advisor is trained to manage portfolios as they grow in size and ensure that different asset categories in your portfolio are allocated properly to achieve your stated goals.

- **Coping with complexity.** IRAs have highly complex tax rules that when maximized can save you or your estate from paying much more than necessary in taxes.

- **Legacy management.** It is the job of your financial advisor, in tandem with an estate attorney and accountant, to smoothly transition IRA assets from one generation to the next, minimizing tax issues and maximizing protection.

- **Laws and loopholes.** No one wants to miss out on tax law changes. Only an educated financial advisor stays up on such changes.

30. How to find the right advisor

If you are serious about planning for retirement, you need a professional financial advisor. Believe it or not, I have found that less than 1% of financial advisors are competent IRA distribution specialists. This means that a vast majority of advisors are not up to speed on IRA distribution rules and are ill-equipped to help you plan using your IRA. Here's how to find the right professional advisor:

- **Stick with certification.** Anyone can call himself or herself a "financial advisor." You want an advisor who at least is subject to professional standards and maintains a level of financial education to meet those standards. These include CFP, CFA, ChFC and CPA. While certification does not guarantee competence, a professional designation does indicate at least a standard of education and accountability.

- **Consider specialties.** Two areas that have a big impact on retirement savings are taxes and insurance coverage. Your advisor should have designations such as CPA (accounting) or CLU (insurance), or have access to experts who do.

- **Focus on knowledge.** A financial advisor should know about the latest IRA rules. He or she also should know how to integrate your IRA into your broader retirement and estate planning. An advisor must show he or she is continually being educated in the specialized tax rules surrounding IRA accounts.

31. Questions to ask an advisor

How can you be sure a financial advisor is up to speed on IRA issues?

Ask the following questions:

1. **How** do you keep up to date on IRA rules?
2. **When** did you last attend an IRA training course? Ask to see the course manuals.
3. **Are** you up on the latest tax law changes?
4. **What** do you recommend I do with my lump-sum distribution from my company's retirement plan?
5. **Who** should be my IRA beneficiary?
6. **How** do you keep track of my IRA beneficiary forms?
7. **What** is my life expectancy and what is my required IRA distribution if I inherit an IRA? What about my beneficiary?
8. **What** will happen to my IRA after I die? How should an inherited IRA be titled and what's the minimum distribution that a beneficiary will have to take?
9. **How** will you integrate estate planning into your plans for my IRA?
10. **Who** will you turn to for help when you need clarification on IRA rules, estate planning and insurance? If the person says he or she knows it all and doesn't have to ask anyone—run.

ED SLOTT'S
ELITE
IRA
ADVISOR
GROUP™
Find an advisor
at **IRAhelp.com**

Paying a fair price for advice

Among the questions to ask a prospective advisor, be sure to ask how he or she will be paid. You'll want to pay enough so you get good advice, but you don't want to overpay. Here are the major modes of compensation for financial advisors:

- **Traditional.** In the days when most financial advisors were known as brokers, they generally earned sales commissions. That's still true—many financial professionals depend on transaction fees to earn a living.

  Although commissions often get a bad rap, this model still makes sense for some investors, particularly for those who intend to hold their investments for the long-haul.

- **Percentage plays.** These days, many financial advisors rely upon fees rather than commissions. Among fee structures, the most common is charging a percentage of assets under management.

  Many advisors believe that this arrangement puts them "on the same side of the table" as their clients. They're motivated to increase your $500,000 portfolio to $600,000 because they will earn more. Similarly, they have a strong incentive to minimize any declines in your portfolio value, as that will decrease their fees as well.

  There certainly are good reasons why this arrangement has grown in popularity. Nevertheless, paying an asset management fee is not the best plan for everyone. If you seldom change your investments or you interact with your advisor infrequently, you should ask yourself if the fee you are paying is really worth it.

- **Alternate arrangements.** Other compensation structures include retainers, in which you pay a flat fee for advice during a specific time period, perhaps one year. Some advisors charge by the hour, just as accountants and attorneys commonly bill for their services. You may even find an advisor whose compensation includes some combination of the arrangements mentioned above.

- **Ed Slott's advice:** Don't be reluctant to ask an advisor about compensation. Get a written explanation and read it carefully to make sure you understand what you'll be paying.

Understand what you'll be getting, too. If you participate in a 401(k) plan, for instance, will that advisor help with those decisions, or will you simply continue what you've been doing? You can expect to pay your advisor in some manner, but you should be confident you'll receive a desirable amount of assistance in return.

32. Is your financial advisor honest?

Just because a financial advisor claims to be certified by a professional organization doesn't mean it's true. In the wake of all the recent financial scandals, it's now clear you have to do a little due diligence on the background of anyone you hire to handle your money.

- **Do it yourself**—Verify that your advisor has actually earned his or her credentials by calling the organizations that award certification. Also confirm with the organization that the advisor continues to satisfy ongoing educational requirements, that complaints have not been filed, and that the advisor has not been disciplined.

- **Hire a pro**—Consider hiring an online background-check firm or agency to verify your advisor's education degrees, any legal cases pending, liens and even dangerous levels of personal debt.

33. Does your advisor speak simply?

One of the most important qualifications of a financial advisor is the ability to explain complex matters simply. No matter whom you hire, eventually that person will be recommending investments for your IRA. If that person is unable to explain what the investment is and the rationale for you owning it, you have a big problem.

- **Ed Slott's advice:** Before you hire an advisor, ask him or her to explain a Roth IRA conversion, an annuity or how IRAs are distributed after death. If you cannot understand the explanation, or the advisor seems to grow impatient with your questions, there may be a communication problem and a big red flag.

34. How to manage an advisor

Even if you choose an honest, educated IRA advisor who understands the distribution and tax rules, and can explain them clearly, you still need to manage your advisor. You're the boss. The advisor works for you—just as though you were running a business. Here's how to keep your advisor on his or her toes:

- **Meetings**—For the first year, request that you and your advisor meet quarterly. Before these meetings, ask for an agenda of items to be covered.

- **Communication**—E-mails sent to your advisor should be answered promptly. Phone calls also should be returned promptly.

- **Statements**—If your advisor has invested your assets through several different firms, request a consolidated statement outlining your IRA portfolio.

- **Accountability**—Ask knowledgeable questions about your advisor's recommendations. Don't assume everything your advisor says is right or ideal. Questions about your assets are also likely to keep your advisor on his or her toes.

- **Pro-active**—Your advisor should not simply present you with advice and then wait for you to respond. Good advisors stay on clients to ensure that necessary steps are taken and decisions are made.

- **Education**—How is the advisor keeping up on the latest IRA tax rules? They are always changing.

35. How to hire the right CPA

Eventually you will need an accountant who is up on current tax laws, understands the best strategies to keep you from overpaying your taxes, prepares your tax returns on time, and has the skills or resources to assist you in the event of an audit.

- **Ed Slott's advice:** The best place to begin your search for a CPA is by asking friends and colleagues for recommendations. Just be sure you're not hiring more CPA than you need and that the person is suitable for someone with your net worth.

36. How to hire an estate attorney

Nearly 60% of Americans do not have estate plans—and most people who do, neglect to update them regularly. Without up-to-date estate plans in place, all of your hard work saving for retirement and hopes to preserve your wealth for heirs are at risk.

- **Ed Slott's advice:** Ask your financial advisor or friends and colleagues to recommend an estate attorney. Make sure the person understands IRA inheritance and distribution rules. The attorney also should understand the rules that govern distribution of assets to trust beneficiaries and heirs by trustees and estate plan administrators.

37. How to hire an insurance agent

Life insurance is an essential part of retirement planning. You may ask, "How can a life insurance policy benefit me if it won't pay out until I'm dead and gone?" While life insurance can be used to provide heirs with appropriate assets when you die, policies can also be used to guarantee heirs a specific sum so you can spend down what you've saved without worrying if there will be enough for them.

- **Ed Slott's advice:** When choosing a life insurance agent, look for someone who is independent or works with a top-rated, reputable life insurance company and can work with your financial advisor. In many cases, your financial advisor may already have an established relationship with an agent or can find one for you.

Chapter 3:
Minimizing Risks

38. Why knowledge leads to wealth

By now you may be asking yourself the following question: "If I've hired a financial advisor, a CPA and an estate attorney, why do I need to read the rest of this guide? Isn't it their job to know all this stuff?" The answer is yes—and no.

- **Ed Slott's advice:** Yes, your advisors should know all of the information in this guide. But as their employer, you need to be up on the best strategies for your needs and raise key issues with them. Smart retirement planning is an ongoing dialogue with advisors followed by action and fine-tuning along the way. The more you know, the better you'll be able to manage the process, protect your interests and prosper in retirement.

39. Big risks to your IRA savings

IRA planning is largely about maximizing the odds of reaching financial goals —and minimizing the risks that your wealth faces. These risks come in all shapes and sizes—including a recession, job loss, costly health crises, an unexpected death and even living longer than expected. Here's how these risks can be reduced:

- **Portfolio threats**—Market and economic risks to your IRA portfolio are offset through proper asset allocation, diversification and hedging.

- **Job threats**—The risk that IRA assets will be needed to pay bills following a layoff can be offset by setting aside enough emergency cash to cover your expenses until re-employment.

- **Health threats**—The risk that your IRA assets will be dramatically reduced to pay for health care is offset with health, disability and long-term care insurance.

- **Legacy threats**—The risk that your death will leave your family without sufficient income over time or that heirs won't inherit what you intended is offset with life insurance.

- **Tax threats**—The risk that your estate will owe more than necessary when you die in estate and income taxes is offset through strategic estate and tax planning.

40. Estate taxes made simple

When you die, the IRS considers all of the assets that are titled in your name or held jointly with your spouse to be part of your estate. The tax law generally allows you to pass all of your assets to your spouse tax-free. But if you die without a spouse, or you've left assets to children and other non-spouse heirs, these assets are tallied up and may face federal and state estate taxes. Such assets include the value of your retirement plans, your taxable accounts, real estate, and all other items of value owned by you.

- **Ed Slott's advice:** To preserve as much of the wealth you've built up as possible and to avoid overpaying your taxes, you and your financial advisor and estate attorney need to take steps to legally minimize the likelihood of taxation.

41. The case of the two Uncle Sams

When you die, your assets pass either to your spouse—or to children and other non-spouse heirs. Who gets what is spelled out in your will and in your retirement account beneficiary forms.

- **Problem:** Most estates will not pay federal estate tax, but some states have a state estate tax. The estate level at which state taxation begins is generally significantly lower. The federal government lets you subtract the amount of estate tax paid to a state from your federal estate-tax liability, up to a limit.

- **Ed Slott's advice:** Talk with your financial advisor and accountant about ways to minimize the impact of federal and state estate taxes. This is often done through gifting and life insurance, for example.

42. Avoid this death-benefit trap

When you take out a life insurance policy on your life, you typically name someone who will receive the cash death benefit when you die. This person is known as the policy's "beneficiary." If the beneficiary is your spouse, no estate taxes will generally be owed. But if the beneficiary is a child or other non-spouse heir, the death benefit will be counted as part of your estate and may be needed to pay estate taxes, reducing the cash payout.

- **Problem:** If you die and your spouse inherits your assets, no taxes are generally owed. But when your spouse dies, his or her much-larger estate will likely pass to your children, increasing the odds of an estate tax.

- **Ed Slott's advice:** While this is not a problem for most individuals in 2016 since the estate tax exemption is $5,450,000 per person and is portable to a surviving spouse, ask your financial advisor and estate attorney about ways to minimize estate taxes when a surviving spouse dies.

43. What is term life insurance?

Term life insurance is the most basic type of policy. You pay a relatively low annual premium for coverage that remains in force for a specific number of years (the "term")—provided the premiums are paid. You can buy a "level term" policy in which the premium stays the same annually for the duration of the policy. Or you can buy annual renewable term, in which the premium starts out very low but inches up annually over the policy's term.

- **Ed Slott's advice:** A term policy typically is ideal for young couples who don't have a significant amount of income and want to maximize coverage and minimize annual premiums.

44. What is permanent life insurance?

The alternative to term life insurance is "permanent" insurance, which remains in force for the duration of your life, not a specific term—as long as the required annual premiums are paid. The premium for a permanent policy is higher than that for a term policy with the same death benefit for two reasons: The policy is in force for life, and part of your premium is deposited into a savings or "cash value" component. There are different kinds of permanent life insurance, so be sure to discuss them with your financial advisor or an insurance agent.

Retirement cash flow from life insurance

Most life insurance policies offer a prime tax benefit. When the insured individual dies, the beneficiary collects a death benefit and owes no income tax. That's true even if the decedent had paid, say, $500 in annual premiums and the beneficiary receives $250,000 or more from the insurer.

Some permanent life insurance policies have cash value. This generates two more tax benefits:

- **Tax-free buildup.** Cash value accumulation is not subject to income tax, inside the policy.
- **Tax-free lifetime cash flow.** The owner of a permanent life policy can withdraw money or take policy loans. This cash flow may be untaxed.

Generally, it takes years for such opportunities to become available. Permanent life policies often have upfront costs that depress the initial cash value. Eventually, sound policies can have substantial cash value, which the policyholder can tap.

Life insurance companies frequently provide "illustrations" to consumers considering permanent life insurance. These illustrations may show years of paying premiums followed by years of untaxed withdrawals or untaxed policy loans, or both. The illustrated cash flow to a living policy owner may be far greater than the premiums paid over time.

- **Ed Slott's advice:** You should buy life insurance because there is a genuine need for the death benefit, such as providing financial support to surviving loved ones. Once you decide to buy life insurance, and how much coverage you need, a permanent life policy might be a good choice if you are in it for the long term. After you have had a permanent life policy for a while and your cash value is substantial, you may decide to supplement your retirement income with periodic policy loans and withdrawals, tax-free. Just keep in mind that accessing your policy in that manner probably will reduce the death benefit.

  Warning! If you tap your policy for retirement cash flow, do so prudently. If you withdraw or borrow too heavily, your cash value may become insufficient and your policy might lapse. Not only would you lose your insurance coverage, you also could owe income tax on the investment earnings that had previously been sheltered inside the policy!

  Your insurance agent should be able to help you keep policy loans and withdrawals within acceptable levels.

45. How to protect your wealth

If the value of your estate is significant and will likely face estate taxes when you die ($5,450,000 for individuals and $10,900,000 for married couples in 2016), consider taking out a life insurance policy to cover the estate-tax tab. The death benefit of this policy will keep heirs from having to dip into the estate (their inheritance) to pay Uncle Sam.

46. Life insurance: Old and/or ill?

When it comes to buying life insurance, don't assume that someone who is old or ill won't qualify for a policy. If you want to cover sizable estate taxes with a life insurance policy, you almost always can secure coverage:

- **Little-known fact:** Some insurers have quotas to fill, and toward the end of each year will issue policies to even old and ill individuals by charging a high one-time premium.

47. Avoid this life insurance trap

To maximize the death benefit of a life insurance policy, don't own it in your name. If you own the policy in your name, the death benefit's value will be included as part of your estate and be subject to estate taxes, reducing the cash your non-spouse heirs will receive.

- **Ed Slott's advice:** Own the policy outside of your estate—perhaps by a trust. By having a trust own the policy, you're still insured and the death benefit will still be available to heirs. Upon your death, the policy's death benefit will pour into the trust—and not be included as part of your estate. Heirs will wind up receiving distributions from the trust based on the trust's terms.

48. Consider a life insurance trust

Many people who amass sizable estates by the time they retire wonder how they can pass as much of it as possible to heirs.

- **Tax traps:** You can't just hand the assets to heirs while you're alive. Uncle Sam can take an enormous bite in the form of a gift tax (visit IRAhelp.com/2016 for the latest levels). On the other hand, if you wait until you die, the assets will be considered part of your estate and may face federal and state estate taxes.

- **Ed Slott's advice:** You can avoid any future estate tax traps by setting up a life insurance trust as the owner and beneficiary of a life insurance policy and naming heirs as the trust's beneficiaries. Then when you die, the sizable death benefit passes into the trust and is excluded from your estate. As a result, your heirs receive every dime you intended for them, not Uncle Sam.

49. Use your IRA to pay premiums

One way to pay a life insurance premium after age 59 ½ is to use your IRA. If you own a Traditional IRA, you'll owe income tax on the amount withdrawn. But the move still may pay since you'll be providing heirs with a tax-free inheritance in the form of the insurance policy's death benefit.

- **Ed Slott's advice:** If you believe that the top tax rates are likely to rise substantially in the years ahead, then it's far more attractive to pay the lower income tax now. Of course, this strategy makes sense only if the funds in an IRA or savings account aren't needed to pay your bills. Also ask your estate attorney and accountant about setting up a life insurance trust.

50. Provide for heirs and spend freely

Many people sacrifice for their kids. But most people go too far, tightening the screws on savings and enjoyment to ensure that heirs wind up with the largest possible inheritance, which is certainly noble. But what if you could leave heirs exactly what you want them to receive—and still enjoy your savings?

- **Ed Slott's advice:** Take a portion of your savings and buy a life insurance policy with a death benefit that covers what you want heirs to have. By doing this, heirs are covered and you're able to spend your savings as you wish. Just be sure to do this as early in life as possible, before health issues emerge and push premium costs up.

51. What's an annuity?

An annuity is purchased through an insurance company and guarantees the owner payments over a set number of years—or until death. An annuity can be purchased with a guaranteed death benefit—which means if you die, your beneficiaries will receive at least what you paid in premiums.

52. What are the annuity types?

There are two basic types of annuities—immediate and deferred:

- **Immediate annuity**—you invest a lump sum, typically at retirement. Regular payments from the annuity start immediately.

- **Deferred annuity**—you invest and your contributions grow tax-deferred, like in a Traditional IRA. You can choose between a fixed or variable deferred annuity, depending on your tolerance for risk. Fixed means your contributions go into investments that earn a fixed rate of interest. Variable means your contributions grow based on market conditions, since they are typically invested in stock and bond annuity funds.

53. Why is an annuity attractive?

An annuity is designed to produce income for its owner in retirement. As a result, an annuity can function like a pension, making regular monthly payments. Such payments keep you from worrying that declining financial markets or the economy will hurt your investment income stream.

- **Ed Slott's advice:** An annuity can be used as a hedge, providing you with a guaranteed income stream that your stock portfolio was supposed to generate but might not if the economy declines.

54. Why buy an annuity in an IRA?

Many advisors frown upon buying an annuity in an IRA, since annuity contributions already grow on a tax-deferred basis. But what if you don't have enough cash in a taxable account to buy an annuity that pays guaranteed income? That's when it may make sense to use IRA assets to buy an annuity within the IRA. Discuss your options with your financial advisor.

55. Aren't annuity fees high?

Admittedly, some annuities tend to have higher fees than other types of investments. But annuities can provide guaranteed income regardless of economic meltdowns and come with a death benefit, so they can't really be compared to most other investments.

- **Ed Slott's advice:** When comparing fees, weigh them against other annuities issued by insurance companies with similar attributes and ratings.

56. Essential estate-planning documents

Most Americans do not have a will or other estate documents. And if they do, the documents aren't likely up to date. What you need an estate attorney to draw up:

- **A will**—ensures that qualifying assets are distributed according to your wishes. It also names a guardian for minor children.

- **Durable power of attorney**—names a family member or friend to make financial decisions for you if you're incapacitated or unable to act.

- **Health-care proxy**—authorizes a family member or friend to make medical decisions if you are incapacitated. Make sure your doctor and hospital have an up-to-date copy.

- **Living will**—states your health-care and end-of-life wishes so the person making decisions knows what you want. Make sure your doctor and hospital also have this document.

- **Medical release**—Often called a HIPAA release (Health Insurance Portability and Accountability Act), this document lets a family member or friend access your medical records to monitor what is going on and make decisions.

Chapter 4:
IRA Strategies

57. Affluent? You can own a Roth IRA

In 2016, if your modified adjusted gross income exceeds $194,000 (couples filing jointly) or $132,000 (single taxpayers), the tax code prohibits you from contributing to a Roth IRA (visit **IRAhelp.com/2016** for all 2016 IRA and tax tables). If your income exceeds these limits, take the following steps to own a Roth IRA:

Step 1: Open a new 2016 Traditional IRA if you don't already have one before April 15, 2017, if you otherwise qualify (see Item 6).

Step 2: Make the maximum 2016 contribution—$5,500 if you're age 49 or younger, $6,500 if you're age 50 or older.

Step 3: Convert funds to a Roth IRA, which you've been allowed to do since the income limit restrictions were waived in 2010.

Step 4: Mind the rules. You'll owe income tax on the conversion if you convert pre-tax funds, and the pro-rata rule will apply if you have after-tax funds in any of your IRAs. You won't be allowed to contribute to your new Roth IRA if your income exceeds the annual IRS limits. Consult a financial advisor or accountant with specialized knowledge in this area.

Step 5: Exploit the loophole. Get around the income restriction by repeating this contribution-conversion strategy year after year.

58. Can Uncle Sam change his mind?

While you can convert a Traditional IRA to a Roth IRA regardless of your income, many people worry that the deficit-weary federal government will change its mind about the tax-free withdrawal status of Roth IRAs.

- **Ed Slott's advice:** Besides the political risks of officials advocating for such a change, Roth IRAs are funded with after-tax dollars. If taxes were to be imposed on Roth IRAs, no one would fund them, boxing the government out of tax revenue. Even if the Roth IRA's tax-free status were to change, existing accounts would likely be exempt from the new rules.

59. IRA conversion? Watch your 401(k)

If you're planning to convert a Traditional IRA to a Roth IRA, delay rolling over a 401(k) from a past employer into your Traditional IRA until the year following the conversion.

- **Reason:** For tax purposes, you want to keep your percentage of nondeductible contributions higher in the pro-rata formula the IRS uses to determine taxation on a conversion.
- **Ed Slott's advice:** You'll need to know which of your past IRA contributions were deductible and nondeductible. Consult your financial planner and accountant before making a move.

60. IRA conversion? Mind your annuity

If you hold a variable annuity in a Traditional IRA you plan to convert to a Roth IRA, have your financial advisor evaluate the annuity's value carefully. You can't use artificially deflated values for variable annuities.

- **Ed Slott's advice:** Get the actual fair-market value of the annuity from the issuing insurer.

61. When to recharacterize a Roth IRA

The IRS allows you to undo a Roth IRA conversion, returning assets to the Traditional IRA.

- **When it pays:** When the value of your newly converted Roth IRA has declined below the value of your former Traditional IRA. The IRS lets you "recharacterize," meaning you can transfer the Roth IRA back to Traditional IRA status—and not have to pay tax on the value that no longer exists. You can always reconvert at a later time.

- **Ed Slott's advice:** If you convert to a Roth IRA, open separate Roth IRAs for each investment category made with the converted assets (stocks, bonds, etc. or U.S. stocks, foreign stocks, bonds, etc.). By doing so, you'll have the flexibility to recharacterize only those assets that have tumbled in value.

Separate Your Roth IRAs

After a Roth IRA conversion, you have a unique opportunity. Until October 15 of the following year, you can recharacterize the conversion, avoid paying the tax, and put the money back in your Traditional IRA. If your Roth IRA has lost value, you'll probably welcome the chance for a do-over.

- **Mixed message:** However, what will you do if some of the holdings in your Roth IRA have gained value since the conversion while others have dropped? You can either hold onto some losers or sacrifice winners that could have provided untaxed cash flow in the future.

- **Ed Slott's advice:** Avoid this problem by converting into multiple Roth IRAs. This can be a simple split (one stock Roth IRA, one bond Roth IRA) or a more involved conversion into Roth IRAs for several asset classes or market sectors. You can even convert into Roth IRAs for individual securities.

For example, suppose you want your Roth IRA to hold only two promising stocks: Alpha and Beta. Thus, you convert $80,000 of your Traditional IRA to two $40,000 Roth IRAs. One holds shares of Alpha Corp. while your other Roth IRA holds Beta Corp. shares.

In this scenario, by October 1 of the following year, the price of Alpha shares is up so this Roth IRA is now worth $50,000. However, Beta shares have dropped, and that Roth IRA is down to $25,000.

At that time, you can recharacterize the Beta Roth IRA. Why pay tax on a $40,000 conversion to own a Roth IRA now worth $25,000?

If you think Beta is a promising investment, at the lower trading price, you can do a reconversion later that year and hold the Beta shares in a new Roth IRA, at a lower tax cost.

- **Let your winners ride.** Meanwhile, you can hold onto the Alpha Roth IRA you already converted. You'll pay tax on a $40,000 conversion and have a $50,000 Roth IRA. If that Roth IRA's value holds up, you can take tax-free withdrawals after five years and after age 59 ½.

  If you had simply converted to one Roth IRA, holding Alpha and Beta shares, you would have converted $80,000 of your Traditional IRA to one $75,000 Roth IRA by October of the following year. Any recharacterization then would mean giving up tax-free Alpha profits as well as Beta losses.

  After you have finished recharacterizing and reconverting the different Roth IRAs, separated by investment type, you can combine them into one Roth IRA for easier management in future years.

62. No life insurance? Convert an IRA

Does a health problem make it impossible for you to qualify for life insurance? Or is a policy's annual premium prohibitively expensive? If you want non-spouse heirs such as children to inherit a sizable sum when you die, consider converting your Traditional IRA to a Roth IRA and naming those heirs as beneficiaries.

- **Reason:** During your life, there are no required distributions from your Roth IRA, and the Roth IRA will pass income-tax free to designated heirs provided five years have elapsed prior to inheritance.

- **Ed Slott's advice:** Be sure non-spouse heirs are named as beneficiaries on the newly converted Roth IRA.

63. Give a grandchild a cool $2.3 million

Most people who own a Traditional IRA assume they will spend down their account over the course of their lifetime. That's because the tax code requires owners of a Traditional IRA to take minimum distributions each year starting at age 70 ½. But here's a secret: The size of that distribution is based on IRS life-expectancy tables, which have you living much longer than standard actuarial tables. That's a good thing—meaning that assets will likely be left over in your Traditional IRA when you die if you take only the minimum required each year.

- **Ed Slott's advice:** Name one or more grandchildren the beneficiary of your Traditional IRA, and their inheritance could turn into millions of dollars. That's because a one-year-old's life expectancy is lengthy, and the amount that must be withdrawn annually from the Inherited IRA will be infinitesimal. So, a $100,000 IRA earning 6% annually will pay that child more than $2.3 million over 80 years.

64. How to set up a stretch IRA

Most people want the wealth they build up over a lifetime to last generations. As noted in the previous tip, if your spouse won't need the assets that remain in your IRA when you die, name your children or grandchildren as the IRA's beneficiary. Then whatever remains in your IRA at death will pass to them. The Inherited IRA will likely grow larger over the life expectancy of those younger heirs. Here's some planning advice you can act on now so your beneficiaries will have more to stretch later:

- **Roll** assets from other retirement accounts into your Traditional IRA.
- **Plan** retirement spending carefully to preserve the assets in your Traditional IRA.
- **Tell** children about the IRA and your plans. Leave them a sealed letter outlining your wishes for them to stretch the Inherited IRA.
- **Or convert** all or part of your Traditional IRA into a Roth IRA—if you have the dollars in a taxable account to pay tax on

the conversion. Why do this? A Roth IRA is more ideal than a Traditional IRA for stretching purposes. That's because there are no required minimum distributions for the original IRA owner. So your Roth IRA assets can continue to grow tax-free for an even longer period since you won't have to withdraw them when you turn age 70 ½.

65. Surviving spouse? Stretch your IRA

If your spouse inherits what's left in your IRA, he or she can set up a stretch IRA for children or grandchildren. What your spouse needs to do:

- **Roll** the inherited IRA into an IRA in their own name. Only a spouse can do this (non-spouses cannot).

- **Name** a child (or other heir) as the IRA's beneficiary. A surviving spouse does this by filling out the IRA's beneficiary form.

- **After** the surviving spouse dies, the assets will be counted as part of his or her estate, which may face estate taxes. The IRA passes to the heir, who must re-title the account as an inherited IRA. Otherwise the IRS could deem it distributed, which would result in income taxes.

66. When to decline an IRA inheritance

When one spouse dies, the surviving spouse is most often the beneficiary of the decedent's IRA. But the surviving spouse doesn't have to accept the inheritance. You have nine months to decline (disclaim) assets meant for you to inherit. Why would anyone decline to inherit an IRA? Here are the main reasons:

- **Assets aren't needed.** A surviving spouse with sufficient assets (or who receives life insurance proceeds) may not need the IRA assets and may want children or grandchildren to inherit them instead. By declining the inheritance, the IRA will pass to the next person named on the IRA's beneficiary form.

- **Estate-tax risk.** A surviving spouse inherits his or her spouse's assets tax-free. But when those assets pass to a spouse, they could result in a much larger estate when the surviving spouse dies, resulting in a stiff estate tax.

- **Ed Slott's advice:** One way to avoid passing along a future estate tax is to decline the IRA inheritance. When this happens, the assets will be counted as part of the decedent's estate and may face estate taxes. Then the heirs next in line as beneficiaries will receive the assets. Those inherited assets can grow large over time if heirs limit their withdrawals only to the required annual distributions. Disclaiming an inheritance is tricky. Before accepting assets, talk to your financial advisor and accountant.

67. Tricky IRA inheritance issues

Leaving assets to your spouse or a single heir is easy. But what if your life is more complicated? Here are three common inheritance scenarios that you should discuss with your advisor and estate attorney:

- **Multiple heirs**—IRA owners who want to pass IRA assets to multiple non-spouse heirs often wonder how to divide the wealth. First, complete the IRA beneficiary form so that all heirs are named. As for the share, dividing the inheritance equally by percentage is often easier and less likely to produce feuds than trying to divide assets fairly by dollars based on heirs' means.

- **New spouse**—People who divorce and remarry need to revisit who they want to inherit their IRA.

- **Single asset**—Naming IRA heirs is relatively simple. You complete the beneficiary form, and assets pass accordingly upon death. But if you are passing a home—an asset that can't neatly be divided—enormous friction can result if you leave heirs to figure out how to share the asset. Ask your estate attorney for strategies to ensure that the property passes equitably and that there are provisions in place for sharing or selling the property and protecting against possible taxes.

68. Steps if you inherit an IRA

The first step is to do nothing. You first want to hire a financial advisor who is educated in IRA strategies and distributions (*see tips #29-34*). Here are the issues you need to discuss with that advisor:

- **Accept or decline**—Just because you are the named beneficiary of an IRA doesn't mean you must accept it. In some cases, declining the inherited IRA may make more sense from a tax perspective.

- **Title properly**—If you accept the inherited IRA and you are not the spouse of the deceased, the IRA needs to be properly titled. It cannot be rolled into your existing IRA.

- **Distributions**—If you're not the spouse, you must take minimum distributions each year based on the IRS' life-expectancy table. Minimum distributions from an IRA inherited by a non-spouse must begin by December 31 of the year following the IRA owner's death.

- **Beneficiary**—You will need to name a beneficiary for your Inherited IRA in case something happens to you. This is done by filling out the inherited IRA's beneficiary form.

- **Ed Slott's advice:** Avoid the temptation to withdraw the entire lump sum you inherit. For one, you'll face income tax on the full amount distributed to you. For another, the longer you leave assets in an account that can grow tax-free, the more you're likely to have over time.

69. Do you qualify for an IRD deduction?

The IRD (Income in Respect of a Decedent) deduction is one of the most overlooked tax breaks available to inheritors of an IRA, 401(k) and other property.

- **How it works:** If you inherit an IRA and take distributions, you'll owe income tax on the amount withdrawn. But if the person you inherited from had an estate that paid federal estate taxes, you are entitled to the IRD deduction, which can range as high as 40%.

- **Ed Slott's advice:** The IRD deduction can save you significant taxes and also is exempt from the alternative minimum tax (AMT). But figuring out your tax savings can be tricky, so consult your financial advisor or accountant.

70. Update your plan as life changes

You now have plenty of actionable, useful information to create a proactive plan to keep more of the money you have earned and make it last as long as you do. But, any plan has to leave room for changes and revisions as new events in your life unfold.

For example, events such as a birth, an illness, a death, an inheritance, a marriage, a divorce, a re-marriage, new grandchild, etc. You get the idea. As situations change in your life, use the information in this guide to adapt and revise your plans, maybe changing a beneficiary or altering your estate plan. Tax law changes also need to be considered since they can have a major impact, especially when it comes to your tax-deferred retirement savings.

- **Ed Slott's advice:** Anticipate change, and when it comes, embrace it and ACT. It is essential to make educated and informed decisions, but they need to be reviewed and often revised to reflect changes in your life or new tax laws. Your plan should always be based on the most current information available.

Chapter 5:
In
Retirement

71. Can you afford to retire?

As you near retirement, you and your financial advisor need to calculate whether your savings will be able to meet your annual needs, which debts need to be paid off, and which accounts you'll turn to first for your post-retirement needs.

- **Ed Slott's advice:** With your financial advisor, make a list of income sources, including IRAs and other savings accounts, Social Security, pensions, etc. Determine how these assets need to be invested to match your risk tolerance and to be preserved for life expectancy. Also, find out how much to withdraw from which accounts.

72. Will your savings last a lifetime?

When you're young, your big goal is to save enough for retirement. When you retire, your big goal is to make sure you don't run out of what you've saved. Most people live longer than they assumed they would.

- **Ed Slott's advice:** Before you retire, consider whether you have enough to sustain your lifestyle during your retirement years. Then take steps to protect against devastating risks to those assets. Talk to your financial advisor about buying annuities to produce steady income for life. You can reduce the cost by buying annuities that don't start making payments until age 85, for example. Also discuss the savings realized if you move to a smaller home and take out long-term care insurance to minimize risks to savings.

73. Pre-retirement advisor questions

1. **How** much will I need to live on each year?
2. **What** sources will fund this amount?
3. **Which** assets should I turn to first if I'm at least age 59 ½?
4. **How** can I increase investment income?
5. **How** much emergency cash should I set aside?
6. **What** debts should I pay off before retirement?
7. **Should** I roll my 401(k) into my IRA?
8. **Should** I convert all or part of my Traditional IRA into a Roth IRA?
9. **How** can I make sure my life insurance policy is on schedule to pay off?
10. **Do** I need long-term care insurance?

74. Watch those nest-egg raids

Retirees who fear running out of assets in retirement frequently wonder how much they can safely withdraw from savings annually to fund their lifestyle.

- **Ed Slott's advice:** A withdrawal rate of 4% per year is good starting point when considering how to draw down your assets without running out of money is a good starting point. Withdrawal rates above 4% will increase the odds of running out of cash. Discuss this with your financial advisor so that all of your income assets are considered and factored into the withdrawal equation.

Playing by the "4% Rule"

The good news is that you probably won't run out of money in retirement, as long as the federal government can transfer electronic Social Security payments into your bank account. The bad news? You may well run short of cash if you live beyond your life expectancy and deplete your portfolio.

To address this concern, financial advisors and academic researchers have come up with what's known as the 4% Rule. Here's the premise:

- **In the first year of your retirement** you should draw down no more than 4% of your portfolio.

- **In each succeeding year,** you can increase your portfolio withdrawal to keep up with inflation.

- **Judging by historic market returns,** this strategy will provide a high probability that your portfolio will last for 30 years or longer.

To put some numbers to this plan, assume that Fran retires with a $600,000 portfolio. In her first year without receiving a paycheck, she withdraws $24,000 (4% of $600,000) from her portfolio for spending money.

Assume that inflation is 3% that year. In Year Two of her retirement, Fran adds 3% ($720) to her annual drawdown, pulling out $24,720.

Suppose that inflation the next year goes up to 5%, so Fran would be scheduled to withdraw 5% more in Year Three, or $25,956. She could round up to a $26,000, to keep things simple.

And so on, year after year. Fran eventually will be withdrawing $30,000 or $40,000 or more in a given year with this plan, depending on how long she lives and the rate of inflation. Nevertheless, it's very likely her portfolio will last as long as she does.

- **Judgment calls.** Keep in mind that there is no penalty for bending the rules. You might, for example, skip the annual inflation increase after a steep drop in portfolio value. Alternatively, you might start with, say, a 5% withdrawal instead of 4% if you plan to eventually sell a valuable home and move into less expensive housing.

  In any case, you should realize that even a 4% withdrawal rate is greater than the current yields from stock dividends and high-quality bond interest. To draw down your portfolio in line with the 4% rule, you probably will have to sell some assets. Ask your wealth advisor to help you develop a plan for liquidating your portfolio assets.

- **Ed Slott's advice:** The main takeaway here is to make sure you have an idea about what size retirement fund you'll need to support your lifestyle. If you would like to withdraw $40,000 a year in your retirement, adjusted for inflation, you'd need a $1 million portfolio, using the 4% Rule. Increased saving may be the only way you can accumulate the desired amount by your retirement target date. Similarly, if you are already in retirement, the 4% rule can help you determine whether or not you may need to adjust your lifestyle in order to avoid running out of money.

75. When to take Social Security

Consider waiting until age 70 to receive Social Security checks. Your monthly payments will be higher than if you began at age 62 or 66, and over a long life the total payout will also be higher. But it is a complex decision, involving other assets, income taxes and estate plans, so it is best discussed with a financial advisor.

76. How to trim wasteful spending

Budgeting is hard for most people—particularly if you don't have a head for numbers or aren't highly organized. Spending is easy when you're younger and employed, because you have income coming in each month. But in retirement, watching where your dollars go is essential. The goal is to make your savings last.

- **Ed Slott's advice:** Make a list of your three types of monthly expenses —*fixed costs* such as utilities; *flexible expenses* such as food and gasoline; and *discretionary expenses* such as entertainment and travel. Get your monthly bills and jot down what you paid. Then add up the monthly total and multiply it by 12 for your estimated annual expenses. Don't forget to include insurance premiums, taxes and any other periodic expenses. Look for ways to reduce costs by saving money on flexible expenses and cutting back on discretionary expenses.

77. Keep savings safe and sound

We know that anything can happen to the economy—and at any time.

The key, clearly, is not to be exposed to excessive risk when you need to preserve your retirement savings.

- **Ed Slott's advice:** Make sure your IRA and other savings accounts are properly allocated for your age and tolerance for risk. In retirement, your biggest risk is defined as running out of money.

78. When to take IRA withdrawals

If you're a retiree who's at least age 59 ½ and unsure whether to withdraw assets from your IRA, talk first with your financial advisor and accountant. Ideally, you want to take withdrawals from taxable accounts first before turning to an IRA. That's because the longer you leave assets in an IRA, the longer they can compound tax-free.

- **Ed Slott's advice:** When you withdraw assets from a Traditional IRA, calculate your tax hit immediately and set aside the cash. Too many people withdraw assets and spend it all. Then when tax time arrives, they don't have the money to pay Uncle Sam.

Avoid early withdrawal penalties

Your IRA is meant to provide retirement income, so there is generally a 10% early withdrawal penalty before you reach age 59 ½. That penalty is added to your regular income tax.

Suppose that Greg, age 52, pulls $10,000 from his IRA. If he is in a 25% tax bracket, he will owe $2,500 (25% of $10,000) in tax. He'll also owe a $1,000 penalty (10% of $10,000), so his effective tax rate on early withdrawals will be 35%.

- **Out of the penalty box.** Fortunately, there are several exceptions to the early withdrawal penalty. If Greg qualifies, he'll owe the $2,500 regular tax but not the $1,000 penalty.

Among several exceptions to the penalty, consider these:

- **Deductible medical expenses.** Suppose that Greg's adjusted gross income (AGI) is $60,000 this year and his unreimbursed medical expenses are $7,500. Greg will generally be entitled to deduct medical costs over 10% of his AGI: $7,500-$6,000 = $1,500. Thus, $1,500 of Greg's $10,000 IRA withdrawal will escape the

10% penalty. This exception applies even if Greg does not itemize deductions on this year's tax return.

- **Health insurance.** Say Greg has lost his job this year and collected unemployment for at least 12 consecutive weeks. He paid a total of $4,800 for family coverage during the year. Greg can withdraw up to $4,800 from his IRA, penalty free.

- **College bills.** In another scenario, Greg pays $5,000 towards his son's college education this year as well as $2,000 so he can take a night school course towards his MBA. If so, he can take up to $7,000 from his IRA this year without owing the 10% penalty.

- **First home.** Greg also can take up to $10,000 from his IRA, penalty-free, to help pay for a first-time home purchase. The money might be used to help Greg's daughter buy her first home or for a home purchase by Greg himself, after going more than two years without owning a home. Note the last part of that sentence. "First-time homebuyer" doesn't have to mean first home, but the $10,000 number is a lifetime cap, not one you can utilize in totality for another home purchase five years down the road.

- **Disability.** If Greg becomes disabled and can't work, IRA distributions escape the 10% penalty.

- **Annuity.** Regardless of whether you are buying a first home or paying college bills or otherwise qualify for an exception, you can avoid the 10% early withdrawal penalty by taking a series of substantially equal periodic payments (SOSEPPs) from your IRA over your life expectancy.

- **Ed Slott's advice:** The SOSEPP rules are included in Section 72(t) of the tax code. By going to an Internet search engine, you can find many 72(t) calculators.

Suppose that Greg goes to an Internet 72(t) calculator and finds an approved method that permits him to withdraw $9,953 a year, penalty-free, from his $300,000 IRA. Greg takes that amount from his IRA and begins a SOSEPP.

A SOSEPP for this purpose must last five years or until age 59 ½, whichever comes later. Thus, Greg—now age 52—must take exactly $9,953 from his IRA each year until he reaches 59 ½. Any departure from this path will result in the 10% penalty being imposed on all of Greg's pre-59 ½ IRA withdrawals, plus interest. Work with your IRA custodian to set up your SOSEPP withdrawals.

79. Retiree tax breaks in 2016

Retirees get breaks on airlines and movie tickets. They also get breaks from the tax code:

- **Capital gains.** If you're in the 10% or 15% tax bracket, long-term capital gains in 2016 are not taxed.

- **Real estate sales.** If you want to sell your home to relocate to a smaller one and you've owned your home for 20 or 30 years, your gain on the sale may exceed the tax exclusions of $500,000 for a couple or $250,000 for a single filer. To avoid capital gains taxes, you need to have big carry-forward losses from last year or sell portfolio losers to offset the gains on the home sale.

- **Reduce your estate.** If you have sizable assets that comfortably exceed what you'll need in retirement, consider making gifts to reduce your taxable estates (visit **IRAhelp.com/2016** for the latest maximum levels). You also can pay education expenses for grandchildren gift-tax free, provided your check is made out to the school. Or you can contribute to a 529 college savings plan.

80. Convert an IRA in retirement?

Much depends on your tax bracket in retirement and whether you have cash on hand to pay the income-tax bill. Starting in 2010, the IRS allowed all taxpayers to convert part or all of a Traditional IRA, a 401(k) or other company plan to a tax-free Roth IRA—regardless of household income! The catch? You have to pay income tax on the fair-market value of the account at the time of conversion. Which means you need the cash to do this.

- **Ed Slott's advice:** Many retirees live longer than expected, making a partial or full conversion extremely tax efficient. That's because the account is likely to grow over time and then pass to heirs tax-free—provided you have had a Roth IRA for five years. Also likely: Your current tax bracket may be higher in the future.

81. Convert an IRA for inheritance?

If you plan to pass your IRA to your children, converting part or all of your Traditional IRA to a Roth IRA likely makes sense. By converting, you will not have to take mandatory distributions starting at age 70 ½. Also, your children will not owe federal income tax on the Roth IRA they inherit provided you have had a Roth IRA for five years. If you're over age 59 ½, you can use the Traditional IRA assets to pay the tax without facing an early-withdrawal penalty. Better yet, pay the tax with other assets.

- **Ed Slott's advice:** If your goal is to pass any IRA to your children, be sure they are named on the IRA's beneficiary form.

82. Beware this IRA conversion trap

If you are age 70 ½ or older and you're already taking required minimum distributions (RMDs) from a Traditional IRA, you cannot dodge the annual RMD by converting the IRA to a Roth IRA. **Rule:** You must first take the required minimum distribution for the year and then convert the remaining Traditional IRA to a Roth IRA.

83. Know the IRA withdrawal rules

Starting at age 70 ½, you are required to begin taking distributions from a Traditional IRA. But how much do you have to take? That depends how you stack up on the IRS' life-expectancy tables. Each year's required minimum distribution is determined by dividing your IRA balance by the number of years the IRS expects you to be around.

- **Doing the math:** Check the IRS life-expectancy table at IRAhelp.com/2016. To calculate your 2016 RMD, find your age.

Then divide the value of your IRA at the end of last year by the corresponding "distribution period." Or ask your accountant.

84. Watch out for retiree scams

Retirees are prime candidates for a wide range of financial scams and schemes. Beware of the following:

- **New advisors**—Always vet a new financial advisor, CPA or lawyer with care by running a background check on their credentials, education and any liens and legal actions pending.

- **Hot tips**—It's very easy to fall prey to advice from friends who claim to have done well with a particular investment. Resist the temptation to get in on the action. In most cases, such ventures may not be right for you and could wind up in disaster.

- **Phone pitches**—Don't be suckered by phone calls from people claiming to represent organizations and asking for personal information. The simple solution is to just hang up.

- **Door sales**—Steer clear of people who show up unannounced with low-cost offers to fix something on your house they've spotted from the street.

- **Social calls**—Beware of pitches from people who use the environment, animals, diseases or other heart-tuggers to hold your attention. Before donating to any charity, check on the charity's existence and make the donation directly through instructions on its website.

- **Pal of a pal**—Watch out for pitches by strangers who claim to be friends of your friends. This is one of the most effective ways to get victims to let down their guard.

- **Fishy e-mails**—Beware of e-mails from banks and financial institutions claiming there's a problem with your account. A real institution would not ask for personal information. To verify your account, never click on the link provided. Always go to your institution's website and access your account that way. Or call the number provided by the institution.

- **Going fast**—Avoid financial pitches that stress there's little time left, or there are only a few opportunities left for those who invest immediately.

- **New friends**—Sophisticated scammers befriend people and spend time developing trusting relationships before pitching a fraudulent deal.

- **Snail Mail**— IRS will always contact you by mail. Beware of e-mails or phone calls that say they are from IRS, especially if they make threats.

85. Run a feud-free family meeting

Unless there's a reason why your children should not know about your finances, a family meeting with your financial advisor is a wise move—especially in retirement.

- **Ed Slott's advice:** Having your financial advisor present and officiating the meeting will keep the summit from sliding into personal issues or being used to settle old scores. By including your advisor, your children will receive a financial education, letting them become more confident managers of their finances and the advisors who are working for you.

86. Secrets of healthy family meetings

When you hold a family meeting with your financial advisor, draft questions and concerns in advance. Your children should know how to contact your life insurance representative, financial planners, accountants, and attorneys. In the meeting, note how the advisors respond to your children. This is a good indicator as to how helpful these advisors will be to your children in the future.

Chapter 6:
Social Security And Medicare

87. What Uncle Sam has to offer

Don't neglect Social Security and Medicare in your retirement planning. The former is a pension from the federal government. You've paid for it throughout your working years so you can collect in retirement. Married couples can generally get two Social Security checks each month.

Medicare is health insurance for seniors, subsidized by Uncle Sam himself. This program is not "Obamacare," as some people call the health insurance law now in effect. Again, you've paid into Medicare as long as you've been working, and a married couple usually gets coverage for both spouses.

- **Ed Slott's advice:** It's true that both Social Security and Medicare are currently expected to run short of money over the long run. However, tens of millions of American seniors (read "voters!") are covered by these programs. Politicians in Washington will continue to tinker with their frameworks, but it's doubtful that benefits will be cut sharply. You can count on some form of Social Security and Medicare to be around when you retire.

Know Your Full Retirement Age (FRA)

When it comes to planning for many Social Security benefits, there's one factor that's more important than just about everything else: your full retirement age (FRA). Many of the benefits you may be eligible for are calculated based on how long before or after your FRA they are received. Plus, there are some more advanced Social Security claiming strategies that can only be used at your FRA or later.

Your FRA has nothing to do with when you actually retire, but rather, it is determined solely by when you were born. So whether you retire at 50 (lucky you!) or you work until 85 (good for you!), your full retirement age is unaffected. Depending upon the year of your birth, your full retirement age may be anywhere from 65 – 67 (although if your FRA is under 66 you should already be claiming any Social Security benefits you're entitled to).

Use this chart to determine your FRA:

Full Retirement Age (FRA)

Year of Birth*	Full Retirement Age
1937 or earlier	65
1938	65 and 2 months
1939	65 and 4 months
1940	65 and 6 months
1941	65 and 8 months
1942	65 and 10 months
1943 - 1954	66
1955	66 and 2 months
1956	66 and 4 months
1957	66 and 6 months
1958	66 and 8 months
1959	66 and 10 months
1960 and later	67

*If you were born on January 1 of any year, you should refer to the previous year. If you were born on the 1st of the month, your benefit—and your full retirement age—is figured as if your birthday was in the previous month.

88. Working and Social Security may not mix

You can start collecting Social Security retirement benefits as early as age 62, but there's a penalty for starting before your full retirement age. If you receive benefits during a year you are younger than your full retirement age for the entire year and you have more than $15,720 of earned income, then you'll have $1 of Social Security benefits deducted for every $2 of earned income you have over the limit. If you receive benefits during the year you reach full retirement age and have more than $41,880 of earned income, then you'll have $1 of Social Security benefits deducted for every $3 of earned income you have over the limit. This only applies to earned income up to the month before your full retirement age. Any deducted benefits will be credited to your account and added back to your Social Security checks AFTER you stop earning more than the limit or reach full retirement age.

- **Ed Slott's advice:** If you're still working before your normal retirement age, it usually doesn't pay to start Social Security. What's more, the younger you are when you start to take benefits, the smaller your Social Security checks will be going forward. Married individuals who start before their normal retirement age may lose the chance to use some sophisticated tactics to maximize a couple's combined income from Social Security.

89. When sooner beats later

If you have stopped working, should you start Social Security at age 62, or soon thereafter? Maybe. It might make sense for one or both of these reasons.

- **You need the money.** With little or no earned income and a shortage of other resources, you might have to start Social Security for cash to pay your bills.

- **Your health isn't great.** By age 62, you might have developed a serious medical condition. Taking the money as soon as possible can make sense, especially if you are single.

If you don't have an immediate need for the money and you're healthy enough to anticipate a long retirement, waiting will increase the size of the Social Security checks you'll eventually receive. Long-term, you may come out ahead. Waiting may work especially well if you're married, and you have earned much more than your spouse over your career.

90. Social Security's 8% solution

If you don't start Social Security at age 62, you can start any time after that. The waiting game ends at age 70, though. There's no point in waiting longer because your Social Security benefits won't increase any more moving forward.

- **Why you should wait.** From age 62 to age 70, your monthly check goes up every month that you practice patience. When all the numbers are crunched, the annual increase is about 8% a year. That's 8% a year, guaranteed by the federal government, with no investment risk. Compare that with what you're getting now from your bank or your money market fund. It's a pretty good deal.

  What's more, that's 8% a year plus any cost-of-living boost. If inflation is, say, 3%, your total annual increase for waiting would be 11% that year.

  To give you an idea of the difference, suppose Al retired at his normal retirement age (66) in 2016. Assuming Al had paid the maximum in Social Security taxes over his career, his monthly Social Security benefit would have been $2,639, or $31,668 a year. But if you make the same assumption about Carol, who retired at age 70 in 2016, her monthly benefit would have been $3,483 a month, or $41,800 a year – and that's not even counting any cost-of-living adjustments!

91. Waiting = longevity insurance

Some people approach the start-versus-wait decision by looking at the break-even calculation. You might say, how long will I have to live for the amounts added to my monthly checks to catch up with the money I didn't receive while I waited? That's one way to make the decision.

Another way is to look at waiting as a means of buying "longevity insurance"—protection against running short of money in very old age. Today, many people are living into their late 80s, their 90s, and even hitting triple figures. That means 25+ years of retirement in many cases, and a real risk of emptying an investment portfolio. At that point, you'll really appreciate receiving a plumper Social Security check.

- **Ed Slott's advice:** The higher-earning spouse should generally wait to receive Social Security if that's practical. When one spouse dies, the survivor will continue to receive the larger of the two spouses' Social Security checks.

Coordinate with your spouse

If you are married, coordinating your own Social Security benefits with those of your spouse is an essential part of making sure you're maximizing the value of the Social Security benefits to which you're entitled. By coordinating your Social Security benefits with your spouse's benefits, you can help maximize income during both of your lifetimes, as well as for the survivor after one of you passes away. For a long time, the file-and suspend and restricted application strategies were two of the most common used by spouses to maximize Social Security benefits. Congress, however, passed a law in late 2015 eliminating these as potential strategies for many Boomers.

- **File and suspend –** Allows you to file for your Social Security benefits, but delay actually receiving those benefits. By doing so, your spouse may be able to claim a spousal benefit on your earnings history (which can only be done if you've filed). However, since you tell the Social Security Administration not to send you your own Social Security benefits, it allows them to continue to earn delayed credits.

  Warning! – You can only file and suspend once you've reached full retirement age or later. Additionally, this strategy will no longer be viable for those requesting a suspension of their benefits after April 2016. As a result of the law Congress passed in late 2015, after that time, your spouse will only be able to collect a spousal benefit if you are receiving your own benefit.

- **File a restricted application** – If your spouse has already filed for their own Social Security benefit or plans to do so, you can file what's known as a restricted application to tell the Social Security Administration to pay you only your spousal benefit. Your own benefit will be unaffected and can continue to earn delayed credits.

  Warning! – You can only file a restricted application once you've reached full retirement age or later. In addition, this strategy will no longer be viable for those individuals turning 62 after January 1, 2016. As a result of the law Congress passed in late 2015, after that time if you file for your spousal benefit, you will also be deemed to be filing for your own benefit. Thus, you would no longer receive any delayed credits if your benefit is more than your spousal benefit.

92. IRAs can play a role in your Social Security decision

As you can see, waiting to start Social Security as late as possible, up to age 70, may pay off. But what if you need more cash flow while you're in your 60s? One approach is to tap your IRA then.

ED SLOTT'S
ELITE
IRA
ADVISOR
GROUP™
Find an advisor
at **IRAhelp.com**

- **Conventional wisdom:** Many financial and tax advisors advocate delaying IRA distributions as long as possible. Required minimum distributions (RMDs) don't start until age 70 ½. The longer you continue tax-deferred buildup inside an IRA, the more wealth you can accumulate.

- **Ed Slott's unconventional advice:** Tapping your IRA during your 60s may be worthwhile if this tactic allows you to defer Social Security. Tax deferral inside an IRA is a real benefit, but this benefit is most valuable when you're in a high tax bracket and owe a substantial amount of income tax.

If you're in your 60s, in need of more cash flow, chances are that you have modest income and a small tax bill. Thus, IRA distributions won't be extremely taxing. Of course, once you're in your 60s, you're beyond the 10% early distribution penalty, which applies to those under age 59 ½.

93. A savvy sequence can slash your 70-something taxes

If you follow the traditional approach (start Social Security in your 60s, begin IRA withdrawals in your 70s), you probably will increase the income tax on your Social Security benefits. Reversing the procedure—drawing down your IRA so Social Security is delayed—can be a tax-saver.

Why? A full explanation would involve delving into one of the most arcane provisions of the tax code, which is saying a lot. Here's the simple version:

- **When you collect Social Security,** some or most of your benefits may be taxed.

- **This tax is determined by a formula.** The formula counts almost all of your income, including IRA withdrawals, but only half of your Social Security benefits.

- **By delaying Social Security,** you'll get a larger check each month. The larger your monthly check of half-counted benefits, the less you'll have to tap your fully-counted IRA for spending money.

- **Doing the math,** accelerating fully countable IRA dollars while delaying half-countable Social Security dollars can mean a smaller tax bill once you start collecting your heftier Social Security checks.

94. Crowding out the tax collector

Under current law, IRA distributions are fully taxed. If you withdraw $10,000 from your IRA, you add $10,000 to your taxable income for the year.

On the other hand, no more than 85% of your Social Security benefits are taxed under current law. If you receive $10,000 from Social Security, no more than $8,500 will be added to your taxable income for the year. Many seniors include less than 85% of their benefits in taxable income because they have moderate income, and some report no taxable benefits at all.

- **Ed Slott's advice:** Any strategy that substitutes Social Security benefits for IRA withdrawals will be a tax-saver. If overall income tax rates rise in the future, as many people expect, this form of retirement income arbitrage will become even more tax-efficient.

95. Make a good idea even better with Roth accounts

As already mentioned, while $1 of IRA withdrawals counts as $1 for determining the taxation of your Social Security benefits, $1 of Social Security benefits only counts as 50 cents. So it pays to load up on Social Security income and reduce taxable IRA distributions.

What's more, withdrawals from Roth IRAs and Roth 401(k)s are best of all: qualified Roth distributions aren't taxable income and they don't count at all on the formula for taxing your Social Security checks.

Say Carl and Donna have $50,000 of Roth IRA distributions a year plus $40,000 from Social Security benefits and no other income. This couple, with no other income, would owe no tax on their Social Security benefits under the formula. Roth IRA distributions are tax-free for taxpayers who are at least age 59 ½ and have held the accounts at least five years.

- **Ed Slott's advice:** Contributing to a Roth 401(k) is one way to get money into tax-free territory while you work. Once you retire, and your tax bracket drops, you can take money from taxable investment accounts to pay the tax on converting Traditional IRA dollars to Roth IRA dollars.

96. Four for the money

Once you stop working, chances are you'll have four possible sources of income.

- **Taxable accounts.** This is money you have in banks, at brokers, or directly in mutual funds. These accounts have a variety of tax treatments. You may receive investment interest and dividends for spending money; you also can sell assets or take withdrawals to raise cash.

- **Tax-deferred accounts.** These include Traditional IRAs, SEP IRAs, and SIMPLE IRAs. You also may have money you kept in an employer plan such as a 401(k) or a pension. For these accounts, withdrawals typically are fully or mostly taxable.

- **Tax-free accounts.** Roth IRAs and Roth-type employer plans such as Roth 401(k)s offer tax-free withdrawals. Typically, distributions are completely tax-free after five years and after age 59 ½.

- **Social Security.** This is a federal life-long pension for workers and their spouses. Depending on the amount and type of your other income, Social Security benefits are tax-free or partially taxable.

- **Ed Slott's advice:** You'll have more disposable income in retirement if you plan to coordinate these sources of future income. The younger you are when you start to plan, the more cash flow you're likely to enjoy.

97. Ed Slott's retirement income plan

After you stop working, you'll need cash for living expenses. Here's a simplified suggested sequence. In realty, some combination of withdrawals across different types of accounts often produces the most tax-efficient results:

1. **Start with your taxable accounts.** In these low-yield times, investment interest and dividends alone probably won't pay your bills. You'll need to take withdrawals and sell assets. Fortunately, taxes on these transactions are likely to be scant.

2. **Move money from tax-deferred accounts such as Traditional IRAs and 401(k)s to your Roth IRA.** Again, these will be taxable transactions, but you probably won't owe much in tax if you're not working or you are in a lower tax bracket. Pay any tax from your taxable accounts.

3. **Draw down your tax-deferred accounts** once you've depleted your taxable accounts. Either use the money for spending or move dollars into your Roth IRA.

4. **Try to wait until age 70 to start Social Security benefits.** Among married couples, it often makes sense for one spouse to start at full retirement age (66 or 67) while the other delays until 70.

• **Bottom line:** The ideal endgame is to go into your 70s with maximum Social Security benefits and all of your savings in Roth accounts. Your Social Security benefits will be untaxed or lightly taxed, under current law, and Roth distributions won't be taxed. Roth IRAs have no RMDs so money you don't need can pass to your beneficiaries, for ongoing tax-free accumulation and distribution.

98. Learn the A-B-C-Ds of Medicare

Generally, Medicare is a great cost-saver. Workers and spouses typically qualify at age 65. Assuming you're not covered by an employer's health plan or by a former employer's retiree health benefits, you should sign up because Medicare offers cost-effective health insurance. There are two main components:

- **Part A.** This covers hospital bills after you pay a deductible of around $1,288 in 2016. For most seniors, there is no monthly charge for Part A.

- **Part B.** This covers doctors' visits and other medical expenses such as lab tests. The Part B premium for most enrollees is about $105 a month in 2016 or less than $1,300 a year. Considering that the over-65 population may incur hefty medical bills this charge generally is a good deal.

- **Ed Slott's advice:** Don't think that Medicare covers all medical costs: it doesn't. You'll still have various out-of-pocket expenses for your health care, and they can be meaningful. Many people buy supplemental "Medigap" policies from private insurers to limit their exposure to medical bills and "Part D" policies to help pay for prescription drugs.

Alternatively, you can join "Medicare Part C," also known as Medicare Advantage, and sign up for comprehensive health coverage through a private company. You won't need a Medigap policy then and you probably won't need a Part D plan, either. Out-of-pocket costs will be limited. The catch, though, is that you'll have to go to certain doctors and hospitals to get the cost savings.

The Medicare website,   , has a find-a-plan feature to help you decide if you want a Medicare Advantage plan and, if so, which one.

ED SLOTT'S
ELITE
IRA
ADVISOR
GROUP℠

Find an advisor
at **IRAhelp.com**

99. Beware of Medicare Part B Premiums

As mentioned, most Medicare enrollees pay about $105 a month for Part B medical coverage. Seniors with higher incomes pay more. The amount depends on your modified adjusted gross income (MAGI). For this purpose, your MAGI is your regular adjusted gross income, plus any (supposedly) tax-exempt interest from municipal bonds or bond funds.

Generally speaking, Medicare Part B premiums are based off of your tax return from two years prior. So, for instance, your 2016 Medicare Part B premiums will generally be based on your 2014 income.

In 2016, the standard Part B premium is $121.80 (or higher). However, most people who get Social Security benefits will continue to pay the same Part B premium they paid in 2015 because there wasn't a cost of living increase for 2016 Social Security benefits.

Here are the MAGI numbers for 2014 (for your 2016 premiums).

File individual tax return	File joint tax return	File married & Separate tax return	Monthly premium
$85,000 or less	$170,000 or less	$85,000 or less	$121.80
above $85,000 up to $107,000	above $170,000 up to $214,000	Not applicable	$170.50
above $107,000 up to $160,000	above $214,000 up to $320,000	Not applicable	$243.60
above $160,000 up to $214,000	above $320,000 up to $428,000	above $85,000 and up to $129,000	$316.70
above $214,000	above $428,000	above $129,000	$389.80

Source: medicare.gov

Those Part B premium numbers are per Medicare enrollee. Thus, if a married couple includes two seniors on Medicare, with MAGI over $428,000, each spouse would owe $389.80 a month for Medicare Part B. That would be a total of $779.60 a month, or more than $9,300 a year for health insurance.

100. Paring Part B premiums

Some planning can hold down your Medicare Part B premiums. The key is to realize that there is a two-year gap between actually receiving that high income and paying the super-premium for medical insurance. Consequently, since you may be eligible for Medicare at age 65, your reported income for every year starting at age 63 may determine your Part B premium. The earlier you start to plan, the better.

- **Ed Slott's advice:** A series of Roth IRA conversions and recharacterizations (reversals) can help you control your Part B premiums. Any Roth IRA conversion can be recharacterized, in full or in part, until October 15 of the following calendar year.

Suppose Marge and Nick are 63 years old. Marge converts her Traditional IRA to a Roth IRA in 2016 when that account is worth $200,000. In 2017, when their accountant prepares their 2016 tax return, they learn that a $40,000 Roth IRA conversion would keep their MAGI for 2016 under $170,000, and thus exempt from the extra Part B premium.

Marge then recharacterizes $160,000 of her Roth IRA conversion back to a Traditional IRA. That leaves a $40,000 Roth IRA conversion for 2016. Marge and Nick can repeat this tactic, year after year, gradually moving more of their Traditional IRA money to the Roth IRA side. Trimming their Traditional IRAs will reduce future taxable distributions and cut their exposure to higher Part B premiums.

Future Roth IRA distributions won't count in this MAGI calculation and thus won't expose them to higher Part B premiums.

101. Appealing excessive Medicare premiums

As you can see, there's a time lag in imposing higher Part B premiums. What if you were working at age 63 or 64, earning a substantial amount, but retired by 65 or 66, with a much lower income? Can you ask for relief from the steep premium payments?

Yes, in some cases. If your income has gone down due to certain specific situations, you can ask for a lower premium. Those situations include:

1. You married, divorced, or became widowed.

2. You or your spouse stopped working or reduced your work hours.

3. You or your spouse lost income-producing property due to a disaster or other event beyond your control.

To support your claim, be ready to produce documentation, such as a death certificate or a letter from your former employer about your retirement.

102. Don't ignore the "health care IRA"

Before you reach Medicare age, you may be able to open a Health Savings Account (HSA). If so, an HSA can provide exceptional retirement planning opportunities, acting as an IRA for health care. HSAs can be extremely beneficial because they offer triple tax savings:

- **Tax-deductible contributions.**
- **Tax-free buildup** inside the HSA.
- **Tax-free distributions** for qualified health care expenses.

In order to have an HSA, you must have a qualified health insurance policy. Such policies have high deductibles, so you'll have low insurance premiums but ample out-of-pocket exposure before the insurance kicks in. With acceptable health insurance, you can contribute to an HSA—depending on your age and the coverage you have, deductible contributions might be over $7,750 a year.

If you wish, you can tap your HSA to pay medical costs right away. There are no time limits on withdrawals, though, so you can keep your HSA intact, growing untaxed, and use it for a tax-free source of cash to pay medical bills in retirement, including prescription drugs and qualified long-term care services.

- **Ed Slott's advice:** Some observers believe that HSA contributions should be Step Two in your retirement planning each year, right after making 401(k) contributions that your employer will match. The triple tax benefits of HSAs are cited to support such assertions. That strategy may or may not be best for you, depending on your personal circumstances, but it is true that you'll probably incur significant health care expenses after you reach age 65. Being able to pay those costs with pre-tax money would be a significant benefit.

Chapter 7:
Required Minimum Distributions

103. Taking money from Traditional IRAs

When you have a Traditional IRA, there are two key milestones to keep in mind.

- **Age 59 ½.** Before then, you'll usually owe a 10% penalty on distributions, in addition to regular income tax. Some exceptions to this penalty apply, such as withdrawals for deductible medical expenses. Other retirement plans, such as 401(k)s, also incur this 10% surtax on early withdrawals, but the rules and the exceptions are not exactly the same as the IRA rules.

- **Age 70 ½.** Now you must take required minimum distributions (RMDs) from your Traditional IRA and, usually, from other retirement plans as well. However, if you are still working and own less than 5% of the company, you don't have to take RMDs from your current employer's retirement plan at that time, if the plan allows this.

What's more, if you have put money into a Roth IRA, you never have to take RMDs from that account, at any age.

- **Ed Slott's advice:** If you need the money, you can withdraw more than your RMD amount—it's a required *minimum* distribution. You can also take distributions from your IRAs at any age, but try to wait until you are at least 59 ½ to avoid the 10% penalty. If you must tap your IRA even earlier, ask your tax pro if there's a penalty exception you can use.

104. Time your RMDs correctly

You're usually required to take RMDs once you reach age 70 ½, but that doesn't mean you must start exactly six months after your 70th birthday. Technically, the deadline is April 1 of the year after the year you reach that magic age. The tax code manages the feat of turning one day into over a year!

Suppose Betty was born on June 30, 1946, so she will be age 70 ½ on December 30, 2016. Betty must start RMDs from her IRA by April 1 of 2017, the following year.

Also suppose that Betty's neighbor Carol was born on July 1, 1946, so she won't be age 70 ½ until January 1, 2017. In this scenario, Carol doesn't have to start RMDs until April 1, 2018. Because of one day's (maybe only a few hours') difference in when they were born, Carol can wait a full year later to start taking RMDs.

Subsequent RMDs are due the following December 31, and every December 31 after that. Betty, in our example, must take her first RMD by April 1, 2017, and her second RMD by December 31, 2017, less than nine months later. From then on, she must take her RMD by every December 31, as long as there is money in her IRA.

Carol starts a year later than Betty, but Carol will be on a similar schedule for RMD deadlines.

- **Ed Slott's advice:** You may not want to wait until April 1 to take your first RMD. If you do, you'll have two RMDs in the year you begin, and that "doubling up" might push you into a higher tax bracket.

In the Betty example, she can take her first RMD in 2016, rather than wait until April 1, 2017. That will give her one taxable RMD per year and may allow her to stay in a lower tax bracket.

105. Calculate your RMD

The amount of your RMD generally depends on two things: your age and the amount in your IRA. Here's how you typically calculate it:

1. Look up the IRS Uniform Lifetime Table. You can find it at **irahelp.com/2016.**

2. Find your age as of December 31 of the year for which the RMD is due.

3. Find your life expectancy (in years).

4. Divide your life expectancy into your prior year-end account balance to find your RMD for the year.

In the example above, Betty reached age 70 ½ at the end of 2016 so she must take her first RMD by April 1, 2017. That's her RMD for 2016, the year in which she had her 70th birthday. Thus, her first RMD will be determined by age 70 on this IRS table.

On the Uniform Lifetime Table, at age 70 an IRA participant has a life expectancy of 27.4 years. If Betty had $100,000 in her IRA on December 31, 2015, she would divide $100,000 by 27.4 to get $3,650: that's the RMD Betty must take by April 1, 2017.

106. Be leery of illiquid assets

Many investors have turned away from stocks (volatile) and bonds (low-yielding) in recent years. They might look for alternatives to hold in their IRAs, and IRS regulations permit many types of IRA investments, from real estate to private businesses.

- **The catch:** Stocks and bonds and other traded securities are easy to value for the purpose of determining RMDs. You simply look at the traded prices on December 31 of each relevant year.

That's not always the case with illiquid assets, such as the medical office building bought inside your IRA. Nevertheless, the IRS requires the IRA custodian to put a value on all IRA assets and RMDs must be calculated based on that value, after age 70 ½. The cost of a valuation is paid by the IRA.

If the set value is too high, you'll withdraw too much from your IRA, pay too much in tax, and sacrifice untaxed wealth accumulation inside the account. However, if the set value is too low, you'll under-withdraw and take insufficient RMDs. This will expose you to a steep penalty, as explained below.

- **Ed Slott's advice:** If it's practical, consider eliminating hard-to-value assets from your IRA before age 70 ½, so RMD valuation won't be an issue. Otherwise, consult with a tax pro to work out a valuation plan that will pass muster with the IRS.

107. Take your RMD—or else!

The R in RMD stands for Required, and the cost of ignoring this requirement is steep. Any shortfall is subject to a 50% penalty!

Suppose Betty has an initial $3,650 RMD, as illustrated prior. If she takes only $3,000 from her IRA by the deadline, Betty will be $650 below the minimum so she'll owe a $325 penalty: 50% of $650. If Betty takes no RMD at all, the penalty will be 50% of the entire $3,650 RMD, or $1,825.

Moreover, those are the penalty amounts. Betty is still required to take her missed RMD, and report the taxable income from her IRA distribution in the year in which she takes the distribution.

108. Let your custodian do the counting?

As you can imagine, determining your RMD can involve a substantial amount of number crunching. Any mistake might generate a too-small RMD and a 50% fine for any insufficient distribution.

IRA custodians are required to send out letters to IRA owners early each year, calculating their RMD for the year or offering to do so. However, using the number provided by the IRA custodian could be a mistake. The custodian will generally only use the date of birth they have on file for you and the Uniform Lifetime Table to calculate your RMD. If your spouse is more than 10 years younger or if your date of birth is wrong, the calculation they do for you will be wrong. It never hurts to double check their math. After all, look where their math got them during the housing crisis!

- **Ed Slott's advice:** If you expect to use your RMD for spending money during the year, arrange with your custodian for monthly transfers from your IRA directly into your checking account. If that's not the case, waiting until year-end to take your annual RMD in a lump-sum will extend the time for potential tax-deferred buildup inside your IRA.

You should be aware that IRA custodians report to the IRS, too, so the tax collectors know who must withdraw from their IRAs. IRS may soon step up efforts to catch taxpayers who neglect this requirement to move money from one pocket to another.

ED SLOTT'S
ELITE
IRA
ADVISOR GROUP™
Find an advisor
at **IRAhelp.com**

109. Mix and match IRA RMDs

Many people have more than one IRA. If so, you must calculate the RMD for each IRA to come up with your total RMD. Then you can take that RMD from any or all of your IRAs.

For example, suppose Art has one large IRA, another with $8,000 and yet another with $5,000. By adding up the RMDs from all three accounts, Art determines that he must take a total of $20,000 in RMDs this year.

Art decides to empty the two small IRAs, for a combined distribution of $13,000. Now, if he takes $7,000 from his large IRA, Art will have met his RMD for the year. Going forward, Art won't have to deal with paperwork from his two small IRAs; he will have only the large account, from which he will take all future RMDs.

If you have a SEP IRA or a SIMPLE IRA, you include that account among your IRAs when aggregating RMDs. However, you can't include inherited

IRAs in that calculation—they need separate RMDs (more about inherited IRAs below). And you can't combine IRAs with employer plans for aggregating RMDs.

- **Ed Slott's advice:** Unless you have a special reason to keep multiple IRAs, consider consolidating them when you reach the RMD stage, or drawing down any small accounts. This will make your life simpler in your 70s and later years.

110. Don't take your spouse's RMD

Among married couples, both spouses may have their own IRAs. Thus, when both spouses are older than 70 ½, they'll both have RMDs. Such couples should avoid a common error: taking all the RMDs from one spouse's IRA or IRAs.

Suppose that Grace has one IRA while her husband Joe has many IRAs, spread around several mutual fund companies. This year, Grace's RMD from her IRA is $18,000 while Joe's RMD total from all of his IRAs is $14,000.

Joe wants to take the $32,000 total RMD from his collection of IRAs, which will enable him to close out some IRAs and simplify his recordkeeping. After all, Joe reasons, the $32,000 of taxable IRA distributions will be reported on their joint tax return, so the couple will pay the proper amount of tax.

No harm, no foul….and no 50% penalty, Joe believes.

However, Joe is wrong. His reasoning will draw a yellow flag from the refs.

- **Ed Slott's advice:** The "I" in IRA stands for Individual. Each IRA owner should take RMDs from his or her own accounts. If not, the penalty will apply.

In the example above, Joe will have a $32,000 taxable distribution, drawing down his IRAs. Grace will have an $18,000 shortfall, and a 50% penalty ($9,000) for not taking her RMD. IRA beneficiaries also have RMDs and aggregation rules to follow, as explained below.

111. IRA beneficiaries have RMDs, too

As explained previously, IRA beneficiaries have certain rules to follow. In simplest terms:

- **Any IRA beneficiary** can withdraw all of the money from the account, and pay any resulting income tax. (Roth IRA beneficiaries often won't owe income tax.)

- **A surviving spouse who is an IRA beneficiary** can roll the IRA to his or her name. From there, the RMD rules apply as they apply to any IRA owner, starting at age 70 ½.

- **All non-spouse IRA beneficiaries** not covered in the two points mentioned above are subject to RMD rules, even Roth IRA beneficiaries receiving tax-free distributions. Any RMD shortfall will trigger the 50% penalty.

- **Ed Slott's advice:** For maximum tax deferral through RMDs, IRA beneficiaries (other than surviving spouses rolling over the account to their own name) should retitle the account to an inherited IRA. Typically, IRA custodians will have a preference as to the form of an inherited IRA's title. RMDs for named or designated non-spouse beneficiaries should begin by December 31 of the year after the IRA owner's death.

112. IRA beneficiaries have their own RMD table

To take RMDs from an inherited IRA, you'll use yet another IRS table found at **irahelp.com/2016:** the Single Life Expectancy Table. Generally, beneficiaries look up their age in the year following the IRA owner's death. Young beneficiaries may enjoy tremendous wealth building over many decades of tax deferral.

Suppose, for example, that Nancy died in 2015 and left her $100,000 IRA to her grandson Phil. The first RMD is due by the end of 2016, the year of Phil's 20th birthday. On the IRS table, Phil has a life expectancy of 63 years, at age 20. Thus, Phil takes an RMD of $1,587 ($100,000 divided by 63) in December 2016.

As you can see, Phil's RMD is 1.587% of the inherited IRA's value. As long as the IRA's investments earn more than 1.587%, the inherited IRA will continue to grow larger.

Going forward, Phil reduces his life expectancy by one year, every year. In 2017, in our example, Phil will have an RMD that's 1/62nd of the IRA value. In 2018, his RMD will be 1/61st of the IRA value. And so on. For years, the RMD will be a tiny fraction of the IRA amount so a successful investment plan, inside the IRA will enable the account to keep growing. If Phil only takes RMDs and the IRA money is invested well, he might withdraw hundreds of thousands of dollars from the $100,000 IRA he inherited.

113. Surviving spouses get extended life expectancy

Just to make things a little more complicated, the IRS has different rules for a surviving spouse who uses the same Single Life Expectancy Table to take RMDs from an inherited IRA—that is, for a surviving spouse who does not do a rollover to his or her own IRA.

Say a non-spouse begins RMDs from an inherited IRA at age 54 with a 30.5-year life expectancy. Each year, that beneficiary would reduce the life expectancy by one year: the RMD calculations would be 1/29.5, 1/28.5, 1/27.5, etc.

A surviving spouse, on the other hand, has no RMDs until the year their deceased spouse would have been age 70 ½. On top of that, spousal beneficiaries who do have to take RMDs (because their deceased spouse would have already reached age 70 ½) get to "recalculate" their life expectancy each year by looking up their life expectancy factor on the Single Life Expectancy Table. Since the factor often decreases by less than one, this allows for greater tax deferral in comparison to what non-spouse beneficiaries must withdraw.

For example, let's suppose a spousal beneficiary has to take their first RMD in the year they turn age 55. Their factor, obtained from the Single Life Expectancy Table, is 29.6. The following year, the spousal beneficiary would, once again, look at the Single Life Expectancy Table, this time finding a factor of 28.7. The difference between these two factors is 0.9. In comparison, a non-spouse beneficiary only looks at the table once – in the year after the IRA owner's death – and then subtracts one every year thereafter, resulting in a shorter life expectancy.

The longer life expectancy numbers used by surviving spouses produce smaller RMDs, smaller tax payments, and more potentially valuable tax deferral.

- **Ed Slott's advice:** Although most IRA beneficiaries who are surviving spouses will roll over the account to their own name, that's not always the case. A spouse beneficiary who will need to tap the IRA before age 59 ½ is often better off remaining as a beneficiary with an inherited IRA in order to avoid the 10% early withdrawal penalty.

Once the survivor reaches age 59 ½, beyond that 10% penalty, he or she can roll over the IRA to his or her own name. Then they can defer RMDs until their age 70 ½. There is no time limit on the ability of a surviving spouse to execute such an IRA rollover.

114. RMDs for multiple beneficiaries

Calculating the RMD when Mary leaves her IRA to her son John is relatively straightforward. John (or his tax pro, or the IRA custodian) can go to the IRS life expectancy table for beneficiaries and do the math.

But what if Mary leaves her IRA to her son John and her daughter Sue? In such cases, the shorter life expectancy is used. If John is older than Sue, John's life expectancy will dictate RMDs from the IRA Mary left to her children. If John and Sue had a kid sister, Ashley, who was also a co-beneficiary, John's shortest life expectancy would still determine RMDs for that inherited IRA.

- **Ed Slott's advice:** In some situations, this rule is inconvenient and may become extremely costly for some heirs. Therefore, multiple IRA beneficiaries should mark their calendars to meet two key deadlines: September 30 of the year after the IRA owner dies and December 31 of the year after the IRA owner dies.

115. Determine the designated beneficiaries

By September 30 of the year after death, the "designated beneficiaries" will be determined. In some situations, acting before then can be helpful. For example:

- **When a charity or nonprofit organization** is among the IRA beneficiaries. Suppose Al's IRA had been left to the children, Craig and Diane, but it also included Al's alma mater as a beneficiary of 10%. A charity or nonprofit has no life expectancy—effectively the shortest among the beneficiaries—so the IRA would have to be fully distributed in a relatively short time period. In that situation, Craig and Diane would lose some potentially valuable tax deferral inside the IRA.

In this example, Craig and Diane can have the IRA custodian distribute 10% of the IRA account to the university, as payment in full. As long as the university is paid before September 30 of the year after the IRA owner's death, this will remove the college as a beneficiary, leaving only Craig and Diane as designated beneficiaries. Then the children can stretch RMDs over Craig's life expectancy.

116. Beneficiaries can go separate ways

If September 30 of the year after an IRA owner's death is the deadline for designating beneficiaries, what occurs three months later, on December 31? That's the deadline for separating an inherited IRA into multiple inherited IRAs, one for each beneficiary.

For example, imagine an IRA was left to the surviving spouse Barbara (50%), son Craig (25%), and daughter Diane (25%). Barbara rolled over her 50% share before the September 30 deadline, leaving Craig and Diane as co-beneficiaries of the IRA that remained. Assuming the IRA contained $400,000 at the owner's death, Craig and Diane would have an IRA worth $200,000.

Then, Craig and Diane would have until December 31 of that year to separate the account into two $100,000 inherited IRAs. They would both have until that date to take the first RMD from their own inherited IRAs.

- **Ed Slott's advice:** By separating IRAs, each beneficiary gains more control over his or her own account. They can choose their own investments and decide whether to take only the RMDs each year or withdraw larger amounts. What's more, now each IRA beneficiary will be able to use his or her own life expectancy for calculating RMDs.

If Craig is 50 when he starts to take RMDs, he'll take those RMDs over a 34.2-year life expectancy. However, if Diane is 40 at that time, she can use a 43.6-year life expectancy to take RMDs from her inherited IRA. The longer life expectancy may allow Diane to take smaller RMDs, enjoy more tax deferral, and thus build more wealth within her inherited IRA.

117. Trusts have their pros and cons

Some IRA owners name a trust as beneficiary. That is, when they die, their IRA will pass to a trust instead of to one or more individuals.

Example: When Edna Franklin fills out the beneficiary form for her IRA account, she enters "Franklin Family Trust" as her beneficiary. The trust document lists Edna's three children as the trust beneficiaries. A trustee is named who will manage the money inside the IRA after Edna dies and handle subsequent distributions.

- **Advantages:** Leaving your IRA (or any other asset) to a trust can be a good idea if you have an heir who is inexperienced in managing large amounts of money, is likely to squander the inheritance, or has other financial concerns. Suppose Edna's son

Gregg bets (and loses heavily) on ball games, while her daughter Heather is a doctor, exposed to malpractice judgments. With a trust beneficiary, the IRA funds will be safer than if they had been left outright to Edna's children.

- **Drawbacks:** Any trust involves time and money to create and administer. A trust that is named as the beneficiary of an IRA may be able to take RMDs over an extended time period, extending tax deferral, but that will be the case only if the trust meets several criteria set out by the tax code.

Assuming the trust qualifies as a "look-through" trust, RMDs will be based on the life expectancy of the oldest trust beneficiary. Generally, the trust beneficiaries will not be able to split the inherited IRA and take RMDs over their individual life expectancies. Therefore, the younger trust beneficiaries will lose some potential tax deferral.

- **Ed Slott's advice:** Don't name a trust as your IRA beneficiary because you think it offers tax benefits. It doesn't. However, if you have concerns as to how your loved ones will handle the IRA they'll inherit, a trust can provide protection. Be sure to work with an attorney who is knowledgeable about the IRA rules for trust beneficiaries.

118. Still more rules on aggregating RMDs

Some RMDs from inherited IRAs may be aggregated, but that's not always true. In order for you to aggregate these RMDs, you must have inherited IRAs from the same IRA owner.

Scenario 1: Suppose Ron inherited two IRAs from his mother. Each year, Ron will calculate the RMD from each of these inherited IRAs. He can add up the RMDs and take the total withdrawal from either IRA, or both.

Scenario 2: Now suppose it's five years later and Ron inherits an IRA from his uncle. In this case, Ron can still aggregate the RMDs from his mother's IRAs, but he must do a separate calculation, based on his life expectancy at the time, in order to take RMDs from his uncle's IRA.

Whatever the RMD turns out to be, Ron must take the distribution for his uncle's IRA from that inherited account.

Scenario 3: Taking the example one step further, suppose Ron reaches age 70 ½, so he must take RMDs from his own IRA. Again, those RMDs must come from his own IRA; if he has more than one IRA, Ron can aggregate the RMDs and take the total from any or all of his own IRAs. However, he can't take RMDs for his own IRA from the inherited IRAs, and he can't take RMDs for the inherited IRAs from his own IRA.

Common to all scenarios: If Ron doesn't take all the RMDs from the correct accounts, he'll owe a 50% penalty on all the RMDs that were left in place when they should have been withdrawn.

119. Requesting RMD forgiveness

The previous items have focused on taking the right RMD amount from the right place and thus avoiding a 50% penalty. However, there might be circumstances in which you under-withdraw or just forget the RMD altogether. If that should happen, and you're facing a stiff fine, you can ask the IRS to waive the penalty. In order to succeed, you must demonstrate that the shortfall was due to a reasonable error and that you have taken the right actions to make up for your lapse.

You use IRS Form 5329, *Additional Taxes on Qualified Plans (Including IRAs) and Other Tax-Favored Accounts* to report the missed distribution and to calculate the penalty. To request a waiver, you must fill out the form and attach a letter of explanation.

- **Ed Slott's advice:** When you submit Form 5329 with a letter requesting a waiver of the penalty, don't include payment for the 50% penalty. IRS no longer requires that payment be sent in with the form.

120. Making up missed RMDs

Before you file Form 5329 to request a waiver of the 50% penalty, you should actually take all the required distributions you've missed, as soon as you make the discovery of an RMD shortfall. Do the calculations, or have your tax professional do them, and move all the RMD amounts from your IRA to your taxable bank or investment account.

Suppose you missed a $10,000 RMD for 2014 and a $12,000 RMD for 2015. You should withdraw a total of $22,000 from any or all of your Traditional IRAs in 2016, thus incurring $22,000 of taxable income for 2016. Of course, you should be sure to also take your 2016 RMD by year-end.

- **Ed Slott's advice:** Assume that an IRS examiner will scrutinize your request for a penalty waiver. Therefore, you should do everything you can to help the IRS agent understand what you have done to correct your error.

  One possible approach is to ask your IRA custodian for separate checks that match each missed RMD. In the above example, you could ask your custodian for a $10,000 IRA distribution and a $12,000 distribution from your IRA with no taxes withheld. Make photocopies and then deposit the two checks into a taxable account.

121. File all necessary forms

If you owe penalties for multiple years, you must file a Form 5329 for each year in order to get a full waiver. These can be forms you file alone or ones that you file with an income tax return.

Previously, we gave the example of missed RMDs in 2014 and 2015. In such a situation, you should file two Forms 5329, one for each of those years. You can file a solo Form 5329 for 2014. If you have not yet filed your 2015 income tax return, you would attach Form 5329 for that year (or both years) to the tax return. Either way, attach a photocopy of the relevant distribution check to the Form 5329, showing that you have received that year's belated RMD from the IRA custodian.

- **Ed Slott's advice:** You shouldn't file an amended tax return as part of your request for a penalty waiver. Once you've missed an RMD for, say, 2014, you can't go back in 2016 and withdraw IRA money for 2014. Instead, you'll take a makeup RMD in 2016, report that withdrawal on your 2016 tax return, and pay tax on that amount of income.

122. Conquering Form 5329

Requesting a waiver on Form 5329 doesn't require an advanced degree in computer science, but it's not child's play, either. Making a common mistake can be costly.

The danger lies in Part VIII of the form, labeled "Additional Tax on Excess Accumulation in Qualified Retirement Plans (Including IRAs)." Here's how to sidestep the trap:

- **On line 50,** enter the amount of the RMD that you were required to take.

- **On line 51,** enter the total of IRA distributions that you actually took during that calendar year.

- **On line 52,** enter "zero," and write "RC" (for reasonable cause) in the margin. Do not enter the amount of the RMD you missed.

- **On line 53,** enter "zero" again.

- **Ed Slott's advice:** The instructions for line 52 of Form 5329 can be confusing, but you should be sure not to put any number on that line. If you put any amount there, you won't get the waiver you're requesting. Instead, the IRS will impose the 50% penalty tax and request payment in full.

123. State your case for a penalty waiver

When you file Form 5329, requesting a waiver of the 50% penalty for a missed RMD, be sure to attach a waiver request. Emphasize that you have taken an IRA distribution equal to the missed RMD, as evidenced by the attached copy of the distribution check from your IRA custodian.

Your statement also should include an explanation for missing the RMD. Unfortunately, the IRS has not issued any notices or rulings that would indicate what's considered to be a good reason for getting a penalty waiver.

- **Ed Slott's advice:** Just saying "I forgot" is not likely to get the penalty dismissed. You'll need to show a reasonable cause. Here are some explanations that the IRS might accept:

  1. Illness or death in the family.
  2. Failure on the part of your IRA custodian, which didn't inform you of your RMD.
  3. Failure on the part of the Post Office, so notices about RMDs never reached you.
  4. Problems with a reputable tax preparer.
  5. Exceptional stress, which might involve a divorce, a lost job, a home foreclosure, the closing of a family business, etc.

In any event, your statement should apologize for the inadvertent oversight, point out that the missed RMDs have been taken, and promise to make every attempt to make all future RMDs on time.

124. Charitable thoughts about RMDs

RMDs generate unwelcome taxes, but a missed RMD generates a steep penalty, and there is no sure way to have that penalty waived. What's more, taking an RMD inflates your adjusted gross income (AGI), and a higher AGI can have expensive consequences throughout your tax return. Just to name a couple of examples, a higher AGI can cost you medical deductions and prevent you from deducting losses from investment property.

- **Now for the good news:** Fortunately, there is a way to satisfy your RMD requirement without getting snared by all these tax traps. You can utilize a tax break called a qualified charitable distribution (QCD). Here's how it works:

Suppose Ellen is 75 years old, with an RMD from her Traditional IRA of $20,000 this year. Ellen, who is charitably inclined, chooses to transfer $20,000 from her IRA to her favorite charity this year. That $20,000 can be a QCD, satisfying her RMD and absolving her from the 50% penalty. It's true that Ellen won't get the usual tax deduction for this charitable donation, but it's also true that Ellen won't have to include that $20,000 distribution in her AGI, and that exclusion can have multiple tax-saving benefits.

- **Ed Slott's advice:** Just as we were going to print, Congress passed a law permanently extending the QCD provision. Prior to this change, the QCDs had been approved by Congress for only short stretches at time before expiring. Each time it expired, Congress renewed the provision retroactively, but often not until very late in the year, making tax planning with any certainty very difficult. That's no longer an issue. The QCD is here to stay, so if you're charitably inclined and are 70 ½ or older, give this strategy strong consideration each year.

QCDs are especially valuable to seniors who (a) have an IRA and (b) take the standard deduction on their tax return, so they don't deduct charitable contributions. Such IRA owners get no tax benefit from their donations so they might as well make them from their IRA and avoid the taxable income from their RMDs.

125. Breaking down the QCD tax break

Now that the QCD is a permanent part of the tax code, it's even more important to know how to make one properly. Here's what you need to know:

- You have to be at least age 70 ½ as of the date of the transfer to use the tax break.
- IRA beneficiaries as well as IRA owners over age 70 ½ can make QCDs, which will count as RMDs.

- The annual limit is $100,000 of QCDs per donor, so a couple in that age range can donate up to $200,000 ($100,000 each) from their respective IRAs.

- Your IRA custodian must make a payment to the charity or charities you designate, not to you. Public charities and nonprofit organizations (colleges and museums, for instance) generally are acceptable recipients.

- Donations to a donor-advised fund, a private foundation, or a supporting organization won't be acceptable as a QCD.

- The charitable recipient must receive your name and address, so it can send you the required acknowledgment. This letter should state that it received the money and did not provide you with any benefit in return.

Chapter 8:
2016
Tax Update

New Publications from IRS

There is now further evidence to our long-standing belief: the IRA rules are incredibly complicated. Last year, the IRS felt that there was so much IRA information to explain, that it split its publication explaining the IRA rules into two separate publications!

What used to be Publication 590, *Individual Retirement Arrangements (IRAs)* is now:

- Publication 590-A, *Contributions to Individual Retirement Arrangement (IRAs)*

- Publication 590-B, *Distributions from Individual Retirement Arrangement (IRAs)*

- **Ed Slott's advice:** It's great to take an active role in your retirement planning and reading for self-education can be a great way to help expand your knowledge base, but there's no way to replace the qualified advice of a knowledgeable professional.

Big Changes to Social Security Planning Strategies

On November 2, 2015, the Bipartisan Budget Act of 2015 was signed into law. The law made several dramatic changes to Social Security planning. Most notably, the law eliminates two tried and true methods that helped many retirees squeeze every dollar possible out of the Social Security system.

Under the law, the file-and-suspend strategy – which can only be used if you've reached your *full retirement age* – is eliminated, effective for suspension requests submitted 180 days after the signing of the act and beyond - which would be around the beginning of May 2016. Instead of family members being allowed to receive a benefit off your earnings record after you've merely *filed*, the law makes it necessary for you to actually be *receiving* benefits for them to do so.

If you were planning to use the file-and-suspend strategy as part of your planning, but will no longer be able to, you will now face a more difficult choice. On one hand, you could hold off receiving your own benefit until as late as age 70. That would make your benefit as large as possible, but would prevent other family members from receiving benefits based on your earnings until that time. On the other hand, you could begin receiving benefits sooner. That would reduce your benefit, but would also allow other eligible family members to claim a benefit off your earnings record sooner.

Another popular strategy, the restricted application strategy, is also being eliminated. Under the Social Security rules, you may be eligible to receive a retirement benefit based on your own earnings record and a spousal benefit based on the earnings record of your husband or wife. At full retirement age or later, you've been allowed to file a restricted application and essentially tell Social Security "pay me only my spousal Social Security benefit, not my own retirement benefit." Those using this approach have been able to receive some Social Security benefits, while still allowing their own retirement benefit to earn delayed credits until as late as age 70. At that time, a switch to their own, higher, benefit was possible.

Now, however, thanks to the Budget Act, if you turn 62 after January 1, 2016, you will no longer be able to file a restricted application – at full retirement age or later – to apply solely for your spousal benefits, while allowing your own benefit to continuously compound and grow. Instead, you will be deemed to be simultaneously applying for both your retirement and spousal benefit, regardless of when you apply.

If you are age 62 or older by January 1, 2016, you are grandfathered into the old rules. If you're not grandfathered into those rules, you will be forced to either wait until as late as age 70 to receive a higher benefit, but receive nothing in the interim, or begin receiving smaller benefits sooner. Neither option is as attractive as the previous restricted application strategy.

- **Ed Slott's advice:** If the Budget Act's changes to Social Security will impact your claiming strategy, update your retirement plan to reflect those changes. Figure out how you are going to make up that lost income or, if necessary, plan to reduce expenses.

myRA Retirement Account Now Widely Available

On January 28, 2014, President Obama announced the myRA, a new type of retirement account, to the American public in his annual State of the Union Address. For about a year, a pilot program allowed certain employers to offer the myRA account to their employees through voluntary payroll deductions, but if your employer did not participate, you weren't able to establish and/or fund a myRA account on your own. That changed late last year.

On November 4, 2015, the Treasury Department announced it was making the myRA available to everyone. Now, while employers can still allow their employees to fund myRAs through payroll deductions, you can do so via direct deposits from your bank account or even directly with all or a portion of your federal income tax refund.

Never heard of the myRA? Here's what you should know:

- The myRA is a special type of Roth IRA. That means that all normal rules for Roth IRAs will apply to myRAs. For instance, myRA contributions will be limited to $5,500 for 2016, or $6,500 for 2016 for those age 50 or older. In addition, the Roth IRA contribution income limits will apply, so if you're a single filer with modified adjusted gross income (MAGI) in excess of $132,000, or a joint filer with MAGI in excess of $194,000, for 2016, you will be prohibited from making any myRA contributions for 2016. Furthermore, myRA contributions will be coordinated with the overall annual Roth and IRA contribution limit, so you cannot fund both a Roth IRA and a myRA with $5,500 each, since the overall limit is $5,500.

- Contributions may be withdrawn at any time tax and penalty free. You can generally withdraw earnings tax and penalty free as well after five years and the attainment of age 59 ½

- A myRA account can have a maximum balance of $15,000 or a lower balance for up to 30 years. When either of these limits is reached, the money must be transferred to a private Roth IRA. You can also voluntarily transfer or roll over your myRA to a private Roth IRA at any time.

- myRAs will be invested in a new United States Treasury security, which will earn interest at the same variable rate as investments in the government securities fund for federal employees. This investment is backed by the United States Treasury and the account carries no risk of losing principal.

- Accounts can be started and continuously funded with very small contributions. The myRA website says that contributions of just $2 will be allowed. Yes, $2! Plus, the myRA has "no cost or fees."

- **Ed Slott's advice:** The biggest beneficiaries of the new myRA will be young savers just starting out in the workforce and those with very modest incomes who can't afford to save much, but who also cannot afford to lose anything.

To learn more or to establish a myRA visit the Treasury Department's website at **www.myra.gov.**

Supreme Court's Landmark Decision for Same-Sex Couples

In the landmark Obergefell case released during the summer of 2015, the United States Supreme Court ruled that the U.S. Constitution requires that states license same-sex couples to marry and recognize same-sex marriages lawfully performed in other states in the same manner that they perform and recognize opposite-sex marriages.

Same-sex couples who were legally married under state law were already recognized as married for federal tax purposes after the *Windsor* case in 2013 and subsequent IRS guidance. However, that decision still allowed states to prohibit same-sex couples from being married or to prohibit recognizing same-sex marriages that were legally performed in other jurisdictions.

In *Obergefell*, the Supreme Court took it a step further. States still are vested with the rights to determine marriage law, but they can no longer discriminate against same-sex couples.

The *Obergefell* decision relates to married couples only. Domestic partnerships and civil unions do not get the same treatment, even if they were afforded rights similar to married couples under state law.

More same-sex couples now have access to spouse-only benefits such as:

- Spousal contributions and the ability to use the Joint Life Expectancy Table to calculate RMDs.
- Spousal rollovers and the special rules for spouse-owned inherited IRAs.
- Qualified plan benefits, including spousal protection under ERISA and the QDRO exception to the 10% penalty.

- Certain Social Security benefits that were previously denied to them if they married in a state that recognized same-sex marriage, but lived in a state that did not.

- Married-joint tax rates (although that can sometimes cause a higher tax). Married same sex couples MUST file either married-joint or married-separate federal returns, but they can no longer file as two single individuals.

- Key estate planning benefits, such as favorable estate and gift tax treatment, enhanced guardianship and adoption rights, and greater ability to make medical and end-of-life decisions.

- **Ed Slott's advice:** Most new laws, court cases, etc. make planning more complicated, but that's not the case with the Obergefell decision. Instead, the decision makes planning for same-sex couples simpler, by making it more like planning for opposite-sex couples. Same-sex married couples can take advantage of all federal tax planning benefits for married couples that are covered in this guide.

Expanded 10% Penalty Relief for Certain Public Safety Officials (Twice!)

- The Trade Priorities and Accountability Act of 2015 – yes, a trade bill – included a provision that will allow more public safety officials to take early distributions without penalty from more of their government-sponsored retirement plans.

- Early distributions from retirement plans are generally subject to an IRS 10% early distribution penalty. However, there are a number of exceptions to this penalty. Of course, not all exceptions apply to all types of retirement plans.

In prior years, the law provided an exception to the 10% early distribution penalty for withdrawals from governmental defined benefit plans if those withdrawals were made by certain state and local public safety officials, such as state and local policemen, firemen and EMS workers, after separating from service in the year they turned age 50 or later. This is commonly referred to as the "age 50 exception."

Changes in the summer of 2015 by the trade bill expanded the definition of "public safety official" to include not only state and local public safety officials, but also certain federal public safety workers, including federal law enforcement officers and firefighters, certain customs officials, border protection officers and air traffic controllers.

The extenders bill, passed in December 2015, added certain nuclear materials couriers, or any member of the U.S. Capitol Police, Supreme Court Police or diplomatic security special agent of the State Department to that list. All of these changes are effective for 2016.

- Eligible employees must still separate from service in the year they turn age 50 or later.

- Beginning in 2016, distributions from both governmental defined benefit and defined contribution plans will qualify for the exception.

- **Ed Slott's advice:** It's generally best not to tap into retirement funds early, but if you do need the money and this new exception to the 10% early distribution penalty applies to you, it's good to know that you can access your employer plan retirement funds penalty free. The funds you withdraw of course are still taxable, but no 10% penalty if you qualify for the new exception.

Qualified Charitable Distributions (QCDs) Are Back... "Forever"

As noted earlier in this guide, the extenders bill brought back qualified charitable distributions retroactively to January 1, 2015. Perhaps more importantly, it also made them a permanent feature of the law. Of course, "permanent" means something different to Congress than it means to you or I. To us, permanent means, well... permanent. Not to be changed. Ever. To Congress, it just means the way it is until they decide to pass another law to override it.

Enhanced Retirement Plan Portability with Roll-ins to SIMPLE IRAs

SIMPLE IRA accounts – a type of IRA-based employer plan – are subject to some weird rules. One of them is that, for the two-year period beginning when contributions are first deposited into a SIMPLE IRA, the funds can only be rolled over to another SIMPLE IRA. No other retirement account money you might have is subject to the same restrictions.

Now, as thanks to the extenders bill passed into law in December 2015, that two-year period will take on even more importance. After your initial SIMPLE contribution has "marinated" in your account for the two years, you will be able to roll any other eligible retirement funds you may have into the SIMPLE IRA as well. Up to this point, only SIMPLE IRA funds were allowed to be rolled into a SIMPLE IRA. This change could be beneficial if, for instance, your current employer offers a SIMPLE IRA and you'd like to consolidate accounts from previous employers to one place.

More Time to Roll Over Bankrupt Airline Payments

The December 2015 extenders bill may also give you more time to rollover a qualifying payment from a bankrupt airline. This is a provision of the law that only really applies to you if you were a participant in the American Airlines pension plan when it filed for bankruptcy in 2011. The law doesn't explicitly state "American Airlines," but rather discusses airlines that "filed [for bankruptcy] on November 29, 2011." Needless to say, that's a fairly limited class of companies and it's clear who Congress was talking about.

If you're the proverbial needle in the haystack here and this applies to you, the law allows you to roll over any or all of the payments into a Roth IRA (as a taxable Roth conversion) within the 180-day window following the passing of the bill, December 18, 2015. Conversely, you are allowed to roll up to 90% of the payments over to a traditional IRA (as a tax-free rollover) within the same time frame.

Notes

Notes

Notes